D0446164

New Zealand

Berlitz®
New Zealand

Original text by Catherine McLeod
Updated by Jane Wynyard
Edited by Christopher Billy
Photography: All photos by Jon Davison, except
for pages 33, 40-41, 59, 78, 101 (New Zealand
Tourist Board)
Cover photograph by Jon Davison
Photo Editor: Naomi Zinn
Layout: Media Content Marketing, Inc.
Cartography by Raffaele Degennaro
Managing Editor: Tony Halliday

Twelfth Edition 2003

CONTACTING THE EDITORS
Every effort has been made to provide accurate information in this publication, but
changes are inevitable. The publisher cannot be responsible for any resulting loss,
inconvenience or injury. We would appreciate it if readers would call our attention to
any errors or outdated information by contacting Berlitz Publishing, PO Box 7910,
London SE1 1WE, England. Fax: (44) 20 7403 0290;
e-mail: berlitz@apaguide.demon.co.uk

010/312 REV

CONTENTS

● A (☞ in the text denotes a highly recommended sight

New Zealand

NEW ZEALAND
AND ITS PEOPLE

Diverse, verdant New Zealand packs an astonishing variety of experiences, scenery, and climatic zones into a relatively compact area. A little larger than the United Kingdom and about two-thirds the size of Japan or California, New Zealand offers attractions both challenging and tranquil — everything from tandem parachuting and bungee-jumping to floating on subterranean streams through caverns illuminated by thousands of tiny glow-worms.

The North Island's steaming volcanic zone and bubbling thermal pools contrast with the South Island's mirror-still, glacier-fed lakes. These two islands comprise over 99 percent of New Zealand's territory. On either of them, you can sip cappuccino in a stylish city café and then, just a couple of hours later, trek through forests so primeval you almost expect to encounter dinosaurs. You can put your feet up in an opulent lodge and enjoy stupendously scenic surroundings while sipping crisp local Sauvignon Blanc and contemplating a foray to the local stream to catch trout.

Most visitors gain their first glimpse of New Zealand as their aircraft approaches Auckland. They view an almost unbelievably green land, bordered by sea curling around broken shorelines, thundering onto great stretches of deserted beach, or idling peacefully into sheltered inlets and calm bays.

New Zealand stands alone midway between the Equator and the South Pole, one of the world's purest and least polluted environments. More than 1,000 km (620 miles) of ocean stretch in every direction: the continent of Australia sprawls 2,250 km (1,398 miles) to the west; the icy wastes of Antarctica stretch 2,300 km (1,425 miles) to the south.

New Zealand is largely hilly, in spots ruggedly mountainous. The north is subtropical, with slow, tidal estuaries, stands of native trees, flourishing orange and kiwifruit orchards, and sweeping beaches. The rippling dunes of Ninety Mile Beach stretch to land's end at magnificently desolate Cape Reinga, revered by the Maori people as the "leaping-off place of the spirits." Rotorua's lake country hisses with thermal steam and bubbling mud. Tranquil as an English garden, the territory overlooking Hawke's Bay on the east coast is a verdant parkland of poplars, weeping willows, and pastures kept in perfect trim by thousands of sheep.

On the South Island, the snow-clad Alps, which extend 650 km (400 miles), are topped by the constantly changing majesty of Mt. Cook, the "Cloud-Piercer" of the Maoris. The far south is a remote and virtually uninhabited terrain of forests, fjords, lakes, and waterfalls. Covered in coastal rain forest and largely ignored by tourists, Stewart Island—off the southern tip of the South Island, across Foveaux Strait—is one of the best places in New Zealand for walking and hiking.

About 16 percent of New Zealand's population is of indigenous Maori extraction; the rest are mainly of European descent. Many are descended from intrepid 19th-century settlers who journeyed from Britain to the uttermost end of the earth to carve out a better life for themselves and their families. The Maoris, a Polynesian people whose poetic oral history relates tales of heroic canoe migrations south and east across the Pacific, arrived at least 450 years before the first European spied the New Zealand coast in 1642. European settlers set to work burning the bush and cultivating the soil. They felled centuries-old kauri trees for use as masts, tore at the hill faces to sow grass, and planted gorse hedges which, in the mild climate, took off across the countryside and grew into miniature forests. Inevitable conflict with Maoris over land and other

Island hopper: ferries traverse the gap between North and South Island, making for an easy commute and a great view.

matters flared into warfare. The Maoris battled British and colonial troops with courage, cunning and tenacity, scoring some notable victories.

Bravery notwithstanding, the Maoris were eventually overwhelmed; the 19th century saw their numbers fall from possibly as high as 200,000 to just 42,000, while the European population moved from zero to over 600,000. By the early 20th century, many *pakeha* (European) New Zealanders considered the Maori race doomed to extinction. But pakeha culture failed to wipe out *Maoritanga* (the Maori way of doing things), and in fact, a Maori resurgence that began earlier last century has been steadily gaining momentum. Maoris are now actively asserting their rights and demanding that earlier pacts such as the Treaty of Waitangi (1840) be honored in full. New Zealand is now officially bicultural, and affirmative-action legislation has helped improve the Maoris' position. Relations between the races are generally cordial, intermarriage is common, and the vast majority of New Zealanders have long since accepted that they must live together as one nation.

In a sense, New Zealand's natural environment is bicultural too. Imported Arum lilies now grow wild on riverbanks and in fields, shining ghostly white against the dark background of native trees. Oaks thrive in New Zealand as they do in Devon villages, and a suburban garden is likely to be a delightful idyll of banana plants and roses, cottage hollyhocks and tropical bougainvillea, planted within sight of indigenous trees like the yellow-flowering kowhai, the glossy-leafed karaka, and giant native ferns.

New Zealand has no wild mammals except for introduced

species such as pig and deer, but bird and marine life flourish. The flightless, nocturnal kiwi is the national bird. (Kiwi has come to mean a New Zealander.) There are also plump wood-pigeons, nectar-sipping tuis, fearless little fantails that often dart into the house, bell-birds, iridescent kingfishers, and rare white herons, whose flight, for the Maoris, is charged with mystic significance. While farming and forestry

Maori traditions have survived near-extinction, and continue to flourish.

have traditionally provided most of the country's income, tourism is rising fast. Tourism supports 118,000 jobs, provides almost 16 percent of export income, and is second only to agriculture in its contribution to gross domestic product.

New Zealand's population is about 3.9 million, with some 570,000 citizens claiming Maori descent. Apart from the English, Scots, and Irish, many Dalmatian and Dutch immigrants have settled in New Zealand. About 200,000 Pacific Islanders, especially from the Cook Islands, Western Samoa, and Tonga, add variety to the scene. Recent years have seen many Asian immigrants arrive, most from China. English is the first language, but the Maori tongue, formerly in danger of dying out, can now be studied at school.

Most New Zealanders are well educated. Many are keen travelers and sometimes spend years abroad. New Zealand claims a fair number of prominent sons and daughters for such a small country: from Baron Rutherford, who split the atom, to international opera star Dame Kiri Te Kanawa, to short-story writer Katherine Mansfield, to Sir Edmund Hillary, the first white man to conquer Mt. Everest. Another famous son is award-winning film director Peter Jackson, director of the acclaimed film "Lord of the Rings", who lives in Wellington. Jackson filmed the epic trilogy, using international and local actors and crew, entirely on location in New Zealand. The movie won four Oscars at the 2002 Academy Awards, including awards for best visual effects, best make-up, best cinematography and best original score.

New Zealanders tend to be egalitarian, competitive, and fit. They're also very friendly and down-to-earth. Traditional practicality is one reason why crafts like weaving and pottery flourish. Inventiveness, ingenuity, and self-reliance are valued highly, and the ability to adapt existing materials to new purposes—a true pioneering skill—is esteemed. Femi-

New Zealand's dramatic natural vistas, such as this one at Lake Taupo, will stay with you long after you return home.

nism thrives, deriving its force in part from the nation's rugged, poineering past. New Zealand was one of the first countries in the world to grant women the right to vote, in 1893. In July 2002, New Zealand's second woman Prime Minister, Helen Clark, was voted in for her second term as the country's leader.

New Zealanders are also avid sports enthusiasts. Hundreds of tennis courts, golf courses, cricket pitches, and football grounds dot the land. Horse-racing is almost a national hobby and the highly physical challenge of rugby culminates in the hallowed All Black Team. Everybody seems to jog, swimming is a way of life, and boats are taken as much for granted as cars. The successful defense of the America's Cup yatch race in 2000, galvinised the whole country.

To make the most of your visit, walk the scenic tracks, try the farm holidays, fish the trout streams, fly out to the glaciers. It's a whole natural experience, waiting to be lived.

A BRIEF HISTORY

New Zealand is a young country in every respect. The North Island is still thermally active, as smoldering volcanoes, geysers, and the occasional earthquake testify. While New Zealand's core landmass drifted north from the southern supercontinent of Gondwana over 100 million years ago, volcanoes have played a major part in shaping the land.

For millions of years, New Zealand was inhabited solely by plants and birds. The country's isolation kept it free of mammals, allowing flightless birds to thrive without threat of predators. The kiwi, an oval brown bird with a long curved beak, is the best known of these and has become New Zealand's national symbol. Others flourished too, like the gigantic extinct moa—taller than a man and able to kill with a single peck.

New Zealand's first incursion into the consciousness of humanity was in A.D. 186, when the enormous volcanic explosion that created Lake Taupo in the center of the North Island reddened skies over Rome in the reign of Emperor Marcus Aurelius Commodus Antoninus.

New Zealand remained undiscovered until sometime between 1000 and 1200 A.D. Anthropologists believe Polynesian navigators arrived by canoe in successive waves over that 200-year period, having sailed from a Pacific home they called Hawaiki, most likely an island in the group that now forms French Polynesia.

Long White Cloud

The Maoris, who called their new land Aotearoa ("Land of the Long White Cloud," from its first appearance on the horizon), have their own account of creation and of the migration across the sea. Maori tradition holds that the Polynesian master navigator Kupe was the first to reach New Zealand.

Still an institution: a Maori meeting house presides over the village (or "pa") in Rotorua.

Finding the two large islands deserted, Kupe did not settle but returned to Hawaiki, where he gave directions for reaching the new land.

Maori lore also tells of the eventual "Great Migration" to New Zealand in a fleet of large canoes. Once settled in their new land, the Maoris lived mainly on birds, fish, ferns, roots, and berries, cultivating taro and sweet potato (*kumara*) and supplementing their diet with human flesh. Cannibalism may have arisen from dietary need, there being no animals other than the dogs and rats the Maoris had brought with them. Maoris lived in fortified villages (called *pa*) and engaged in much intertribal warfare. They brought carving to a high art, both of wood and of greenstone, a highly-prized variety of jade.

In pre-European Maori society the tribe (*iwi*), presided over by a chief (*ariki*), was divided into a number of smaller units (*hapu*). Major issues affecting the tribe were debated in the *marae,* or village meeting-place. These terms are still used in New Zealand.

High priests were trained in tribal history and ritual, including the imposition and lifting of *tapu,* a broad term meaning, among other things, "holy" or "forbidden." The concept of *mana* (prestige) was of great importance and often led to war, conducted hand-to-hand with spears, clubs, and throwing sticks. Battles were conducted on a comparatively large scale with high casualties. Prisoners often ended up as slaves and were sometimes cooked and eaten. An affront to a tribe's mana could lead to an *utu,* or vendetta, which could last for generations.

Europeans Stake Their Claim

New Zealand was named by the Dutch explorer Abel Janszoon Tasman, who in 1642 became the first European to sight the territory. Tasman (whose last name has been bestowed on the sea separating Australia and New Zealand) had been sent by the Dutch East India Company to search for the great unknown southern continent, *Terra Australis Incognita.* Shortly after Tasman anchored off the northwest tip of the South Island, a Maori war canoe intercepted a party of his crew rowing ashore. The Maoris killed four Dutch sailors and Tasman named the place Moordeaners (Murderers) Bay. Later settlers preferred a less contentious designation—Golden Bay. Tasman named the new country Staten Landt; the name was later changed to Nieuw Zeeland after the Dutch province of Zeeland.

Over a century passed before renowned English navigator James Cook circumnavigated New Zealand in 1769 and made meticulous maps. Many coastal sites still bear the picturesque names Cook gave them. They include Cape Kidnappers, now the site of a large colony of gannets, and Young Nick's Head, a prominent headland named after the cabin boy on Cook's ship *Endeavour*. Overall, Cook's relations with the Maoris were reasonably cordial. He admired their bravery but found them little inclined to trade. It was Cook who claimed New Zealand for Britain.

Frenchmen Jean-François Marie de Surville and Marion du Fresne sailed in Cook's wake. Du Fresne's encounter with Maoris in the Bay of Islands, north of Auckland, was dramatic, to say the least. The Maoris killed and ate him, along with about 20 of his crew.

News of New Zealand's existence began to attract adventurers—traders, sealers, whalers, and rampaging buccaneers—who based themselves largely around the Bay of Islands. They kidnapped Maoris, broke their tribal laws and introduced disease, firearms, and rum. In retaliation, Maoris killed and ate the crew of two ships. Lurid reports of profligate and degenerate seamen battling heathen cannibals in the South Pacific began to circulate abroad, reaching the ears of the Reverend Samuel Marsden, a zealous clergyman and magistrate in the Australian colony of New South Wales.

Marsden, who had earned the nickname "the flogging parson" for his brutality towards convicts in Australia, set out for New Zealand as a missionary for the Anglican Church Missionary Society. His aim was to convert and "civilize" Maoris, and to save the souls of the various intemperate characters who were preying upon them.

Marsden established church missions in New Zealand and preached the first Christian sermon there on Christmas Day, 1814. But nine years passed before a Maori converted. By this time, firearms were entering New Zealand in large numbers.

Maori chiefs armed their tribes and taught them the art of musketry. Maori hostilities were directed generally not at Europeans but against each other. Guns gave warring chiefs new and more efficient ways of slaughtering tribal enemies. The 1820s and 1830s witnessed horrifying intertribal bloodshed.

Church influence increased and Maoris began converting to the new religion in increasing numbers. A series of atrocities against Maoris and equally ferocious Maori reprisals helped missionaries to persuade a number of influential chiefs to ask the British Government for protection. By 1831, fear of French annexation supplied another reason for Britain to intercede. The English appointed James Busby as "resident," an official position similar to governor. Busby's

The world's largest war canoe, at Waitangi—Maoris defended many an inlet with these intimidating vessels.

declared aim was to reconcile all groups, but he failed to achieve this and in 1838 the office was discontinued. Captain William Hobson was appointed lieutenant-governor and British land in New Zealand was administered as a dependency of the colony of New South Wales in Australia.

Hobson drafted the Treaty of Waitangi, which was signed on February 6, 1840 and has been a source of contention ever since. In essence, the Maoris ceded sovereignty to the British Crown in exchange for law and order and the rights of ownership to tribal lands. Discussion of the treaty and interpretation of its clauses continue to this day. About 50 Maori chiefs signed it initially, and by June 1840 over 450 additional signatures had been collected from outlying districts. Many may not have understood the meaning of their action. The Maoris could not conceptualize the giving away of land, as it belonged to everyone, with occupants changing from time to time.

The treaty gave the British Crown sole right to purchase land. Large-scale European settlement began, fostered by Edward Gibbon Wakefield, who established the New Zealand Company in Britain. Wakefield hoped to establish a utopian colony along the lines of English society, but excluding those on the lowest rung of the social ladder. The company bought land cheaply from the British Government and sold it to settlers, priced at levels that would appeal to the middle ranks of English society (the aristocracy was unlikely to see benefit in emigrating to the end of the world, and the lower working classes could not raise the money). The four years between 1839 and 1843 saw 19,000 British settlers head to New Zealand under New Zealand Company auspices.

Maoris Strike Back

Europeans underestimated Maori attachment to the land. Disputes over it, and over other matters, led to the New

Shantytown, a replica gold-rush boomtown, offers a step back into New Zealand's glittering decade (1861–1870).

Zealand Wars—about 40 years of intermittent battles between Maoris and Europeans. The British Empire, beset by larger and more strategic wars around the world, did not commit significant troops to New Zealand until the early 1860s. Even without these reinforcements, troops outnumbered their Maori opponents in most battles. Skilled guerrilla fighters, the Maoris fought tenaciously, developing a system of trenches in their fortified villages that protected them from artillery.

Tribal allegiances complicated matters, as some Maoris occasionally sided with European forces attacking opposing tribes. The King Movement, started by a chief called Wiremu Tamihana, tried to achieve unity among the Maoris by establishing a monarchy, but the attempt foundered.

"The Beehive" backs a statue of New Zealand's favorite PM, Richard John Seddon.

When the fighting was over, the Maori "rebels" were punished by confiscation of land. The British Crown changed the rules, permitting settlers to buy land directly from the Maoris, who were duped out of yet more land. The *pakeha* (the Maori word for white settlers) acquired the most fertile land, and by 1892 the Maori people were largely confined to just 4.5 million hectares (about 11 million acres), much of it useless for farming.

The Maori population of the South Island has always been much smaller than that of the North Island, a consequence of the Maoris having settled New Zealand from the north. The South Island remained relatively free from conflict. The discovery of gold in the rivers of Otago province by an Australian, Gabriel Read, in 1861 triggered a gold rush. Thousands of immigrants poured into New Zealand and gold became the country's main export. Dunedin—a Scots-dominated commercial and banking center—grew into the country's largest town.

The boom was over by 1870, but for a brief period the Shotover was known as the "richest river in the world." Within a decade, foodstuffs had replaced gold as New Zealand's main earner. The advent of refrigerated cargo ships made it possible to transport meat and dairy products to distant markets, primarily in Britain or other British Empire countries.

The Constitution of 1852, drafted by Governor George Grey, granted a measure of self-government with the introduction of an elected House of Representatives. Six Provincial Councils and the superintendents of the provinces were also elected directly. The British monarch remained the Head of State, and the governor, appointed by London, nominated members of the Legislative Council, who held office for life.

Only individual landholders were allowed to vote in elections held in 1855 and 1856, effectively excluding Maoris, who owned their land collectively. The franchise, slightly liberalized in 1867, was later extended to all men aged 21 and over. Then, in 1893, New Zealand women became among the first in the world to gain the vote—more than a decade before the Suffragettes started campaigning for the same right in Britain.

King Dick at the Reins

For more than ten years, until his death in 1906, a benevolent liberal, Richard John Seddon, served as the country's prime minister. Familiarly known as King Dick, he made New Zealand famous as a humanitarian democracy. In addition to women's suffrage, old-age benefits and compulsory state arbitration in industrial disputes were introduced. Seddon coined the phrase "God's Own Country" (since irreverently reduced to "Godzone") to describe New Zealand.

In 1914, New Zealand entered the First World War on the side of Britain. New Zealand and Australian troops formed the Australian and New Zealand Army Corps (ANZAC) to fight Germany alongside other British Empire soldiers. On 25 April 1915, the Anzacs landed at Gallipoli (now located in Turkey) in an ill-conceived diversionary operation that cost thousands of lives. The carnage, and Anzac heroism during the Gallipoli campaign, had a powerful effect on New Zealand's psyche. Anzac Day (April 25) is a national holiday and day of remembrance.

From Hunger to Humanity

The Great Depression of the 1930s dealt a savage blow to New Zealand, a small country dependent on overseas markets. Exports fell 40 percent in two years, reducing some families to making clothes out of sacking and living on cabbages grown in their gardens. The government slashed public expenditure and unemployed men received the dole only if they took government-organized work. Rioting, looting, and stealing broke out in spots.

When the Labour Party took power in 1935, New Zealand resumed its commitment to equality. It introduced a social security system, comprehensive medical services, and state-financed housing schemes. Maoris became eligible for all these benefits and were given extra help in an attempt to equalize standards of living.

In World War II, more than 140,000 New Zealanders served overseas, in Europe and the Middle East. When Australia pulled back its troops from Europe during the war to deter a threatened invasion by Japan, New Zealand troops continued to serve in Europe. Some 11,000 lost their lives, including New Zealand airmen fighting to defend London from attack by the German Luftwaffe.

In 1947, New Zealand gained the right to amend the Constitution without reference to Britain. The Legislative Council (the upper house of Parliament) was abolished in 1950. Parliament now consists of a single chamber, the House of Representatives; New Zealand is a member of the (British)

Commonwealth; and a governor-general, usually a New Zealander, represents the Queen. There have been recent suggestions that a new flag free of Britain's Union Jack should be adopted, and that the country should become a republic, but they have not gained mass support.

The last two decades have seen New Zealand switch from a socialized economy offering "womb to tomb" benefits to a highly deregulated market economy, producing some friction in the process and an erosion of the country's former egalitarian ethic. New Zealand's rate of emigration has kept population growth virtually static for a generation. "Overseas" is still a magic word, holding promise of better jobs and salaries, of recognition for performers and artists, and a rather more cosmopolitan lifestyle than is sustainable in a country of about 4 million inhabitants.

Waiouru: The QEII Army Memorial Museum with relics from World War II.

A Closer Economic Relationship (CER) between New Zealand and Australia is bringing their economies into alignment. Yet New Zealanders retain their sense of identity, even when abroad for decades. A bicultural pakeha/Maori nation has been forged that retains an international focus but views the verdant hills and seaswept beaches of New Zealand as home.

Historical Landmarks

1000-1200 Maoris migrate by canoe from Polynesia.

1642 Dutch explorer Abel Janszoon Tasman sights and names New Zealand.

1769 English navigator James Cook visits New Zealand and claims it for Britain.

1839-1843 19,000 British settlers migrate to New Zealand.

1840 Maori chiefs sign Treaty of Waitangi.

1845-1872 New Zealand Wars rage as Maoris clash with settlers and troops.

1852 Governor George Grey draws up Constitution.

1855 First elections held.

1861 Gold discovered in rivers of Otago province.

1893 Women granted the right to vote.

1911 New Zealander Ernest Rutherford, the "father of nuclear physics," becomes first man to split the atom.

1914 New Zealand enters World War I.

1915 ANZAC soldiers storm ashore at Gallipoli in disastrous military misadventure.

1930 Depression hits; exports plummet 40 percent.

1935 Labour Party takes power.

1939 New Zealand enters World War II.

1947 New Zealand gains right to amend its Constitution without reference to Britain.

1950 Upper house of Parliament abolished.

1953 Edmund Hillary and Sherpa Tenzing Norgay conquer Mt. Everest.

1984 New Zealand refuses entry to nuclear-equipped US warships and adopts non-nuclear policy.

1995 New Zealand wins America's Cup yachting race.

2000 NZ hosts APEC Summit and America's Cup.

2001 The world premiere of the acclaimed film trilogy 'Lord of the Rings', directed by Peter Jackson.

WHERE TO GO

To really get the feel of New Zealand, try if you can to visit both islands. The **North Island** has a landmass of some 115,000 sq km (71,415 sq miles, about the size of Louisiana). Though it's smaller than the South Island, the North Island has a warmer climate and is home to most of New Zealand's population. At the far northern tip of the North Island is rugged **Cape Reinga**. From there the island arcs southeast to the historic **Bay of Islands,** past the Central North Island's steaming thermal springs, past fiery **Mt. Ngauruhoe** and the skier's playground of **Ruapehu,** down to **Wellington** and **Cook Strait.**

About one quarter larger than the North Island, the **South Island** is a land of noble, rugged landscapes. About 935,000 people live on the South Island (compared to about 2.9 million on the North Island). You can sometimes detect a warm burr in the voices of South Islanders, an inheritance from early Scottish settlers. The main city is **Christchurch,** on the east coast.

To the north of the island lie the **Marlborough Sounds,** a labyrinth of inlets, islands, peninsulas, sea-flooded river valleys, and lushly forested hills. The **Southern Alps** run almost the length of the island in a snowcapped spine, covering an area larger than the Alps of Europe. To the west, lush forests flourish; to the east are wide and fertile plains, terrain that's well-suited to grain farming—and cycling.

In the southwest, **Fiordland** offers New Zealand's wildest and most spectacular scenic beauty. This remote region, a World Heritage area and one of the world's largest national parks, is sometimes called the walking capital of the world. Finally, to the south, New Zealand's third major landmass, **Stewart Island,** exists in such isolation that the world's largest parrot, the kakapo, lived there undiscovered until 1977.

AUCKLAND

Sandwiched between stunning twin harbors and built on 48 volcanoes (extinct, Aucklanders hope), Auckland has long been New Zealand's prime gateway and largest city. Its population topped 1 million a few years ago and growth is proceeding at a pace that indicates one in three New Zealanders will live there within ten years. Urban planners foresee Auckland's population doubling by the middle of next century. Scenic areas such as the Waitakere Ranges to the west, the Hunua Ranges to the south, and Waiwera, Okura, and Puhoi to the north will be maintained as green belts and protected from development.

To the west of Auckland lie the shallow waters of Manukau Harbour, navigable only to small ships. Waitemata Harbour to the east is a "Sea of Sparkling Water," indented with bays and inlets and scattered with islands. One of them, Rangitoto, a volcano active until only 200 years ago (the last major eruption was 750 years ago), stands guard at the harbor entrance.

Auckland is unlike any other city in Australasia, having overtaken Honolulu to become the world's largest Polynesian city. Auckland also has a growing Asian presence, a smorgasbord of multicultural eating places, and a scenically dramatic setting. The city's status as New Zealand's commercial center has been bolstered by a steady migration of corporate head offices from other parts of the country.

Auckland is sprinkled with little bays and harbor views. To the Maori people, the area was *Tamaki-makau-rau,* "the place of a hundred lovers." British administrators, with deplorable lack of flair, renamed it after an English admiral. Auckland has long since dropped its colonial sobriquet of "Queen City" and

Sandwiched between stunning twin harbors and built on 48 volcanoes, Auckland is guaranteed to enthrall.

now prefers "City of Sails." It is said to possess the world's highest number of boats per head of population, and it certainly looks that way each January, during the Anniversary Day yachting regatta, the world's largest one-day yachting event. The race celebrates the foundation of the city in 1840 as capital of the country—a title it lost 25 years later to Wellington.

The city's most striking modern landmark is the recently completed **Sky Tower,** the tallest building in the Southern Hemisphere; a visit to the tower offers an audiovisual depiction of Auckland's history and panoramic views of the twin harbors 328 m (1078 ft) below. Glass-fronted elevators whisk visitors to the top, where a revolving restaurant turns steadily at one revolution per hour. Below the tower, New Zealand's largest casino, Sky City, is thronged with gamblers.

You don't have to be a yachting enthusiast or a Rugby Union fan to enjoy Auckland's sports scene. If you fancy a round of golf, the Gulf Harbour Country Club, 30 minutes north of Auckland on the Whangaparaoa Peninsula (ask a Kiwi how to pronounce it), is built on terrain that course designer Robert Trent Jones described as "one of the truly great sites I have had the chance to work on worldwide."

Finding your way around Auckland isn't difficult, although lack of an urban rail or subway system causes periodic traffic jams. The city's three main freeways (the Northern, Northwestern, and Southern) provide quick access to most parts of the city from various exit points.

Auckland's climate is mild but changeable. Bright sunlight can switch without warning to a downpour. However reassuring the sky may seem in the morning, it's wise to take a raincoat or umbrella when you set out.

Waitemata Harbour (venue of the Anniversary Day Regatta) is New Zealand's largest port. Curving over the harbor, **Auckland Harbour Bridge** links the city to the

City of Sails: Auckland is said to possess the largest number of boats per capita. Here, Harbour Bridge ramp and marina.

North Shore suburbs. You can drive over the bridge or take the ferry to the marine playground of **Devonport,** with its multi-hued Victorian rooftops. Devonport is the start of the **Coast-to-Coast Walkway,** an exhilarating 13-km (8-mile) hike (for the moderately fit) that takes four hours and displays some of the best scenery Auckland has to offer. A succession of beaches loops northward from Devonport up the east coast.

City Sightseeing

Start your sightseeing at the **Ferry Building,** terminus for boats to various points in the Hauraki Gulf. Not far away, at Viaduct Quay, the **National Maritime Museum** displays Maori seafaring relics and yachts, plus an exhibition on the America's Cup. The restored French Renaissance-style **Customs House,** built in 1888 by Thomas Mahoney, is now a nest of boutiques.

Queen Street cuts through the city center from the Ferry Building. The **Town Hall,** a stone edifice at the corner of Grey's Avenue and Queen Street, fronts Aotea Square. The **Central Public Library** (Lorne Street) contains some surprises—Shakespeare's first folio (1623) and the largest collection of Alexandre Dumas manuscripts outside the Bibliothèque Nationale in Paris, to name two.

Auckland City Art Gallery, on Wellesley Street East, exhibits works with a New Zealand connection. Between the Art Gallery and Auckland University's crenellated Neo-Gothic tower, **Albert Park** is a favorite lunch-hour spot for office workers and students. The **Supreme Court** (1868) in Waterloo Quadrant was built to resemble Warwick Castle in England, complete with turrets and gargoyles, each a touch incongruous in a South Pacific setting.

The Domain, a leafy precinct of playing fields and gardens, is Auckland's premier green space. A spring feeds the pond where the country's first rainbow trout were hatched from California stock. The **Auckland War Memorial Museum,** with its extensive ethnological and natural history collection, stands on a rise in the Domain. Museum highlights include an authentic Maori meeting-house (1878), a carved gateway, and a fine old war canoe, 25 m (82 ft) long. Portraits of Maori chiefs by C. F. Goldie (1870–1947), a painter who used an almost photographic style, give a good idea of how Maori nobility looked in the days of early European settlement. Native species fill the Hall of New Zealand Birds. Set aside an hour to see the museum. www.akmuseum. org.nz.

Leaving the Domain by the Parnell Road exit places you in the smart suburb of **Parnell,** once down at the heel, but now a trendy village of boutiques, cafés, and restaurants. The colonial-style bank and the **Cathedral Church of St Mary,** built in 1888 of native timbers, are the highlights.

South of the Domain, **Mt. Eden,** Auckland's highest point, rises 196 m above the city. The Maoris call the volcanic cone *Maungawhau,* "Tree-Clad Mountain." A fortified village stood here as far back as the 12th century. From the summit you can see into the now quiet crater and in all directions over the city.

Another volcanic cone, **One Tree Hill** in Cornwall Park, provides equally panoramic views. Sir John Logan Campbell, the "Father of Auckland," is buried on the summit, not far from an obelisk that he raised in honor of the Maori race. To meet New Zealand's most famous flightless bird and national symbol, the kiwi, visit **Auckland Zoo.** It lays the world's largest egg—one quarter the weight of the mother bird. The zoo's Nocturnal House also houses the slow, awkward tuatara, a lizard-like reptile that has survived without modification since the time of the dinosaurs. www.auckland zoo.co.nz. Alongside the zoo, the **Museum of Transport and Technology** (commonly referred to by its acronym, MOTAT), attracts machinery and invention enthusiasts. New Zealanders, an ingenious and inventive people, flock to it. West of the city center, **Ponsonby** offers restaurants of all ethnic persuasions, plus little galleries and second-hand shops. A pleasant drive along the waterfront takes in Okahu Bay, **Savage Memorial Park** with its monument to Michael Savage, the country's first Labour prime minister, and **Mission Bay,** where the former Melanesian Mission House serves as a museum devoted to Melanesian artifacts.

To see sharks feeding (Tues and Thurs) or local marine life anytime, visit **Kelly Tarlton's Underwater World** at Orakei Wharf, on Tamaki Drive. Moving walkways transport visitors through acrylic tunnels for an undersea view of sharks, rays, fish, and other marine creatures swimming contentedly in converted sewage tanks. Antarctic Encounter is another popular attraction here. www.kellytarltons.co.nz.

Auckland Environs

West Auckland is the source of much of New Zealand's excellent wine. This thriving industry, much of it centered on the Henderson Valley, testifies to the skill of immigrant families from the former Yugoslavia. Many wineries can be visited. Not far away, the **Waitakere Ranges** are a popular walking and picnicking destination; Arataki Visitor Center (Tel: (09) 303-1530) has maps and details. **Karakare Beach,** one of the region's most scenic, served as a backdrop for the opening scene in the award-winning film, *The Piano,* which was directed by New Zealand director Jane Campion.

Hauraki Gulf, site of the country's first maritime park, is a vast area of sheltered water between the mainland and Coromandel Peninsula. Dozens of islands lie within the park's 13,600 sq km (8,450 sq miles). Rangitoto Island, purchased by the Government in 1854 for about NZ$40, is noted for its harsh, volcanic landscape (strong-soled, non-slip shoes are advisable). Kawau Island offers nature walks and a thriving colony of wallabies. Mansion House, once the residence of Governor Grey, stands on the island.

☞ Coromandel

The rugged Coromandel region, about a 90-minute drive southeast of Auckland, has became more accessible since the Pacific Coast Highway was upgraded. Traversing the North Island's wild and spectacular east coast, the highway links the Coromandel, the Bay of Plenty, and Eastland with Auckland and Hawke's Bay. The region is one of New Zealand's most ruggedly beautiful, with waterfalls, secluded hot springs, huge expanses of windswept beach festooned with driftwood, and old gold mines. Seafood along the way is fresh and delicious.

The perfect view: Coromandel Peninsula offers some of New Zealand's most ruggedly spectacular vistas.

In the 19th century, the **Coromandel Peninsula** was exploited for kauri timber, gum, and gold. Stands of forest were axed, but some remain, providing a home for rare species of frog, the North Island crow (korako), hundreds of kingfishers, and seabird colonies (on the offshore islands). Semiprecious stones such as carnelian, agate, chalcedony, and jasper are washed down from the hills into creeks to mingle with the pebbles on the western beaches.

You can stop off at **Waihi,** where New Zealand's biggest gold strike was made in 1878. At Thames, a few hardy prospectors still work their claims, but commercial mining ceased in the 1920s and the area is better known today for its thriving arts community. In Coromandel itself, 56 km (35 miles) north of Thames, artists in residence include potter Barry Bricknell, who built New Zealand's only narrow-gauge railway so he could reach premium potting clay at the top of his property. Thousands of visitors zig-zag up the hill on the little train each year.

If you explore the Coromandel on foot, watch out for old out-of-use mineshafts concealed by undergrowth.

The Whitianga area of Mercury Bay is close to where Maori explorer Kupe is said to have landed. You can drive there via scenic route 309. Hahai Marine Reserve nearby boasts fine white sandy beaches. If you visit Hot Water Beach, where piping hot thermal waters percolate through the sand not far beneath the surface, you can rent a shovel at the general store and dig your own little spa pool, which will fill promptly with therapeutic thermal water. Relax as long as you wish—up to two hours before or after low tide—allowing cooling sea water to mingle alternately with the hot water.

NORTHLAND

Subtropical Northland, a region with a strong Maori tradition, stretches 350 km (190 miles) north of Auckland to Cape Reinga. Sheltered bays like Matapouri, Oakura, and Doubtless Bay fringe the coast; so do dozens of coves (some of them accessible only by boat). Starting at Pouto, on Kaipara Harbour, the way north to the cape is lined by a virtually unbroken series of beaches. Game fishing is a big attraction as is scuba diving, especially around the Poor Knight Islands. Parts of Northland are covered by ancient rain forest, where you can see fine specimens of New Zealand's forest giant, the kauri tree, prized last century for its suitability for ship masts.

The fastest road to the north is east via Waipu and Whangarei. The west coast road bisects Trounson Park and Waipoua Forest, where the towering kauri trees are protected. A good approach to touring the region is to head north by way of Whangarei, returning via Opononi, Omapere, and Dargaville.

Auckland to Whangarei

The slow-paced farming township of **Warkworth,** some 69 km (43 miles) north of Auckland, stands alongside the Mahurangi River. To the east lies **Sandspit,** the terminus for the ferries to Kawau Island, dotted with the holiday homes and boating jetties of Auckland's affluent yachting fraternity.

Whangarei, with a population of about 45,000, is Northland's largest town. Its gardens are renowned and its deep-water harbor is filled with yachts. The country's major oil refinery is situated at Marsden Point (there's a scale model there for inspection). The **Clapham Clock Museum** is an offbeat attraction containing some 1,300 timepieces of widely varying ages, styles, and backgrounds. Whangarei Falls (off the road to Ngunguru) provides three river pools and Whangarei Heads offers relaxing beaches.

BAY OF ISLANDS

The Bay of Islands is one of New Zealand's most historic and scenically striking regions. **Paihia** is the area's most tourist-oriented town, well located as a base for excursions. The town traces its history back to 1823, when the Reverend Henry Williams established New Zealand's third mission station here. *Tui,* a three-masted bark moored at Waitangi Bridge, now serves as **Kelly Tarlton's Shipwreck Museum.** Relics and treasures recovered from hundreds of New Zealand shipwrecks range from Rothschild jewels to a bottle of 1903 whisky.

A cruise on the Bay of Islands is an enchantment not to be missed. You'll find Captain Cook's brief description of this marine paradise—"very uncommon and romantic"—to be accurate. Launch trips include a breakfast cruise, a lunchtime champagne cruise, a long run all the way to Cape Brett and Piercy Island, and the Cream Trip. This last tour is actually a mail run to smaller islands that lasts almost six hours.

This Maori meeting house (whare runanga) in Waitangi is adorned with the carvings of many tribes.

Most cruises visit the Hole in the Rock, a cape at the end of the bay with a deceptive cleft through which ships can pass.

Points of interest in the Bay of Islands include **Marsden Cross,** where Samuel Marsden preached the first Christian sermon on December 25, 1814, and **Moturua Island**. The latter sheltered French explorer Marion du Fresne in 1772, not long before the hapless mariner was killed and eaten by Maoris at Te Hue, along with several of his crew. A monument donated by the French in 1972 commemorates the bicentennial of du Fresne's landing.

Waitangi, separated from Paihia by the Waitangi River, is where the Maoris signed the controversial treaty of 1840, by which the British assumed sovereignty over New Zealand. **Treaty House,** built in 1833 for British resident James Busby, is now a museum. A flagstaff in front marks the spot where the treaty was signed. A commemoration ceremony is held here each February 6, although mass protests by Maori land-rights activists in recent years have made its future uncertain. A Maori meeting-house (*whare runanga*), built for the centennial celebrations in 1940, stands nearby, adorned with carvings from many different tribes. The standing figure (*tekoteko*) at the apex of the roof represents the ancestors of the Maoris who sailed from Polynesia centuries ago. The world's largest war canoe, named after the canoe in which Kupe is said to have discovered Aotearoa, is on display a short walk from the Treaty House.

Russell, across the bay, is quieter and less touristy than Paihia. The two are linked by regular ferry services and road connections. Believe it or not, laid-back, sleepy little Russell was once one of the world's roughest and most dangerous ports, known by the Maori name Kororareka. English evolutionist Charles Darwin, who visited in 1835, found Kororareka a lawless outpost inhabited by "the very refuse of society." Grog and girls were the main attractions.

On Russell's waterfront, the **Duke of Marlborough Hotel,** rebuilt several times, lays claim to holding the oldest liquor license in the country. The handsome Maori Police Station was built in 1870, well after the fire that destroyed most of the town's old buildings.

Pompallier House was built as a print shop for French Roman Catholic bishop of the Southwest Pacific, Jean Baptiste Francois Pompallier, who strove to counter the tracts in

---

The Human Side of Houses

Maori meeting houses are constructed in symbolic human form: the apex of the roof serves as the head, the ridgepole as the backbone, the barge boards as arms, the rafters as ribs, and the space inside as the chest and belly.

the Maori language that were being distributed by rival denominations such as Wesleyans. The Bungalow, next door, was home to James Clendon, first US Consul.

Christ Church, built in 1836, is the country's oldest surviving house of worship. Charles Darwin (a churchgoer for much of his life) contributed money for its construction. A replica of Cook's bark, *Endeavour,* can be found in the **Captain Cook Memorial Museum** on York Street, along with mementos of Kororareka in its wicked old days.

Flagstaff (Maiki) Hill above the town has seen a succession of flagpoles rise and fall. Hone Heke, the first Maori chief to sign the Treaty of Waitangi, chopped down the first flagpole in 1844. Heke grew suspicious of British land interests and resented the government collecting dues from visiting ships—dues that formerly had been paid to him. Outraged by the flagpole felling, Governor Fitzroy observed that the flagpole was "a mere stick, but as connected with the British flag of very great importance." When the flagpole was re-erected, Heke cut it down again. Four times he laid low this symbol of British authority. Finally the dispute came to a head and anti-government Maoris under Heke's command attacked and sacked Kororareka in a battle that saw colonial troops evacuate the settlement. A chance spark, probably caused by British warships firing on Kororareka, exploded a powder magazine and the whole "vile hole" (as a contemporary dubbed the rum-sodden settlement) went up in smoke.

More recently, Maori land activists have emulated Heke several times by chopping the flagpole down. When you visit the site you may or may not see a flagpole standing.

Kerikeri, 25 km (15.5 miles) northwest of Pahia, is surrounded by orchards, mainly orange, mandarin, kiwifruit, and tamarillo. It is set on the Kerikeri Basin, where white-masted boats and dark, encroaching bush give an idea of the magic and romance of old New Zealand. The area is known for its many craft outlets. Graceful **Kemp House,** overlooking the basin and used by early missionaries, is New Zealand's oldest building. It was completed in 1822—another reminder of how young a nation New Zealand is.

The **Old Stone Store,** not far from Kemp House, once served as a munitions store for troops fighting Hone Heke. It later became a shop and a missionary refuge, and has recently been restored. For a taste of pre-European New Zealand, climb up the hill to **Rewa's Village.** This unfortified Maori settlement, known as a *kainga,* has been reconstructed in authentic style.

Cape Reinga

The best way to reach Cape Reinga is to take one of the modified buses that thunder along Ninety Mile Beach. The trip from Paihia on the Bay of Islands takes about 11 hours. Rental cars are specifically *not* insured for this drive, in part because smaller, non-four-wheel-drive vehicles often get bogged down in sand and sometimes even submerged by the tide. (Local farmers are happy to haul them out with tractors—for a fee.)

No matter how you choose to reach the cape, the drive definitely has its rewards. The great arc of Ninety Mile Beach is so impressive you may not think of questioning its length (it's actually only 60 miles). The surroundings are wildly beautiful, with ocean on one side and pale, storm-fingered dunes on the other.

Cape Reinga itself, a place of powerful Maori spiritual significance, falls 5 km (3.1 miles) short of being the country's northernmost point (that title belongs to Surville Cliffs). The cape can be so windy at times that you can hardly stand up straight. Black rocks and screaming gulls mark the end of the land. Rippling into the distance is the line where the Tasman Sea meets the Pacific Ocean, while far out, barely visible, lie the Three Kings Islands.

CENTRAL NORTH ISLAND

If you head south out Auckland down the southern motorway to the Rotorua thermal area (a common touring route) you will pass through Ngaruawahia, former center of the Maori King Movement. **Turangawaewae Maori Village** is the official residence of the reigning Maori monarch, to whom a number of tribes swear allegiance and government representatives offer their respects on ceremonial occasions. The monarch's role has considerable social and cultural significance. On Regatta Day, (the closest Saturday to March 17), the village is open to the public and canoe races are held.

The city of **Hamilton,** center of a rich dairy-farming and agricultural region, began life as a British military settlement on the banks of the Waikato River. The Waikato Museum of Art and History combines the once separate history museum and gallery.

☛ Waitomo Caves

Outcrops of stratified and eroded limestone mark the

Waitomo Caves, with its galaxy of glowworms (and other lurkers...).

approach to Waitomo, honeycombed by a network of caves and underground galleries. Three caves are open to the public on guided tours, complete with commentary.

Glowworm Cave (a river runs through it) was known to the Maoris from antiquity. European settlers were amazed by the magical beauty of the Glowworm Grotto, described by one observer as "a fairyland without fairies." Today you view the grotto from a boat, pulled across the river by a fixed wire beneath galaxies of glimmering luminous pinpoints. Visitors are warned to stay silent; the slightest sound dims the brilliance of the thousands of bluish lights that illuminate the darkness and reflect in the inky water below.

New Zealand Highlights

Milford and Routeburn Tracks: These two trails are among the most spectacular. Each offers guided walks with comfortable accommodation. (See pages 91 and 92)

Coromandel Peninsula: About a 90-minute drive southeast of Auckland, the Coromandel is one of New Zealand's most ruggedly beautiful regions. (See page 32)

Bay of Islands Cruise: Captain Cook called this region "very uncommon and romantic"—and he was right. Take a boat trip and don't miss the Hole in the Rock. (See page 35)

Waitomo Caves: European settlers described the magical beauty of these glowworm-illuminated grottos as "a fairyland without fairies." (See page 41)

Rotorua: Surging geysers, bubbling mud pools, steaming gardens, and strong Maori traditions distinguish Rotorua. Whakarewarewa is its best-known thermal area. (See page 43)

Kelburn Cable Car: An essential trip for visitors since 1902, it now costs NZ$3.00 round-trip and runs 7am-10pm weekdays and 9am–10pm weekends and public holidays. (See page 55)

Nelson/Marlborough Wine Tours: Many wineries have tasting rooms and restaurants; (See page 98)

Hagley Park in Christchurch: The biggest city on the South Island offers over 3,000 hectares of parks and playing fields. (See page 66)

Franz Josef and Fox Glaciers: The most accessible and largest of 60 glaciers in Mt. Cook National Park, these rank among the scenic glories of New Zealand. (See page 70)

Bob's Peak, Queenstown: The Skyline Gondola zips up Bob's Peak (446 m (1,462 ft) in four minutes) for superb views of Queenstown on the shores of Lake Wakatipu, one of the world's most dramatically scenic spots. (See page 73)

Fiordland National Park: A hauntingly beautiful world of wild valleys, soaring mountains, and startlingly blue water. (See page 76)

The glowworms are larvae of a mosquito-like fly (*Arachnocampa luminosa*), unrelated to the European glowworm beetle and rare outside New Zealand. With tail-light glimmering, the larva swings to and fro in a kind of gossamer hammock, letting down sticky threads to catch the midges that breed in the water. The adult fly is rarely seen.

Nearby Aranui Cave, named after its Maori discoverer, is dry, with illuminated stalactites and stalagmites. Ruakuri Cave, said to be named after a pack of wild dogs (*kuri*), is open for increasingly popular black-water rafting, which involves donning a caving suit and floating through pitch-black caverns in a rubber inner tube. You can also rappel into the caves. For caving insights, visit the **Museum of Caves,** which has an information center inside the front entrance.

Rotorua

The distinctive, thermal, rotten-egg smell of hydrogen sulfide gas proclaims your approach to Rotorua, nicknamed "Sulfur City." Here steam drifts up from drains and private gardens; even the golf course has thermal hazards. Residents have harnessed some of this natural energy for central heating and swimming pools. Concrete "steam boxes" in suburban gardens are used for preparing outdoor feasts.

Rotorua is a major center for Maori culture—one third of the city's population is Maori. *Marae* (tribal meeting places) dot the area. You can see Maori artisans at work in the Maori Arts and Crafts Institute at **Whakarewarewa** (usually called simply "Whaka" by the locals), 2 km (1.2 miles) south of the city center. Visit St. Faith's Anglican Church in Ohinemutu Maori Village on the shore of Lake Rotorua for its remarkable pews, pulpit, and altar, all enriched by traditional Maori carving. Etched into the chancel window is a depiction of Christ wearing the feathered cloak of a Maori chief, placed so that the figure appears to be walking on water. Services here are held in Maori, and the singing is superlative.

Government Gardens, aptly known to the Maoris as *Whangapiro* ("Place of Evil Odors") is a British colonial creation that has been immaculately maintained. Within it, Tudor Towers (1907), formerly a fashionable spa center, now operates as a museum and art gallery. For a thermal soak, try the therapeutic **Polynesian Pools** at the eastern end of Hinemoa Street, a mostly open-air complex of about 30 pools. The Lake Spa section is the most private and exclusive. Sulphur Point, behind Tudor Towers, is a lakeside bathing spot in sight of Mokoia Island.

The best-known thermal area around Rotorua is at Whakarewarewa. Here, **Geyser Flat** features seven active geysers. Pohutu (Maori for "splash") is the star, gushing several times a day on average, sometimes to over 30 m (98.4 ft). Adjacent pools and mud-pots bubble pungently, some plopping like porridge, some weirdly colored. Never stray off the paths to get a better view: the ground is a mere crust in places and the water is scalding. The same applies to all thermal areas: they are safe as long as you take the warning signs seriously.

To see what a pre-European fortified *pa* looked like, visit **Rotowhio,** a replica of a traditional Maori village. The gateway is carved with the embracing figures of Hinemoa and Tutanekai, two lovers from a local Maori legend. (The legend is so well known that anyone in Rotorua should be able to relate it to you.) Maori carvers can be seen at work in the nearby the Arts and Crafts Institute.

Organized excursions to **Waimangu Volcanic Valley** are comprehensive and worthwhile. Some walking is involved; but you can arrange transport to avoid it, and provision can be made for visitors in wheelchairs.

The valley was created in 1886 when Mt. Tarawera exploded with such force that flashes of fire were seen as far away as Auckland and reverberations were heard in Christchurch, 650 km (404 miles) to the south. Ash blackened the air, and mud and lava engulfed houses and buried the Pink and White Terraces, a delicate thermal accretion considered to be one of the natural wonders of the world. The terraces are now submerged beneath Lake Rotomahana, which swelled to 20 times its previous size.

Eleven days before the eruption, an old Maori priest (*tohunga*) reported sighting a ghostly war canoe paddling across Lake Tarawera. The Maoris in the area took it as an omen of impending tragedy. Curiously, two separate parties of Europeans also claimed to have seen the phantom canoe. Fact or fiction, the Tarawera area is so sensationally savage that even skeptical visitors tend to agree that much of it should be regarded as *tapu* (sacred).

The Waimangu trip takes in a walk through places of thermal interest to Lake Rotomahana, a launch trip across the lake, and a short walk to Lake Tarawera. This is followed by a second cruise that includes a visit to the buried village of Te Wairoa, New Zealand's equivalent of Pompeii, surrounded by incongruously well-trimmed lawns. Return via the Blue and Green Lakes, tinted striking colors by underground mineral deposits.

Several trout springs run down to Lake Rotorua. **Rainbow Springs Trout and Wildlife Sanctuary** is the best known. All the springs feature trout swimming freely, tame enough to be hand-fed. If you want to try some fishing, contact Tourism Rotorua (1167 Fenton St.; Tel: 07/ 348-5179; www.rotorua-nz.com) for information.

Fabulous views of the city and lake can be enjoyed from the restaurant atop **Mt. Ngongotaha,** which you can acce by cable car or chair-lift and leave by luge toboggan or a

Wairakei wonders: the silica terraces of Orakei Korako, one of New Zealand's most impressive thermal areas.

ing-fox aerial cable-way. The **Agrodome at Ngongotaha,** on the northern outskirts of Rotorua, tells you all you want to know (perhaps more than you want to know) about New Zealand's sheep. You can even pet them. The display is more interesting than it sounds; try to catch a sheepdog show. When the people of Rotorua yearn for sea and sand, they usually drive to the beach and surf resort of **Mt. Maunganui** on the east coast. In holiday high season (Dec–Feb) a ferry links "the Mount" to the prosperous Bay of Plenty harbor town of Tauranga, an hour's drive from Rotorua.

Wairakei

Wairakei, 74 km (46 miles) south of Rotorua, marks the cen-
~r of an active volcanic zone extending some 241 km (150
~es) from Mt. Ruapehu through Taupo and Rotorua to

White Island, New Zealand's only continually active volcano, in the Bay of Plenty. Wairakei once boasted over 20
geysers, but geothermal electricity generation has tapped the
steam, so only mud-pools survive. A visitor center close to
the road near at the power project explains how it works.

The road from Rotorua to Wairakei, running south from
Whakarewarewa, provides good views of **Rainbow Mountain**
(just past the Waimangu turnoff). The rock-face is tinted in delicate pink, beige, and cream, and rare plants abound in the area.

Watch for the signposts to Waiotapu, the site of Lady Knox
Geyser and Champagne Pool (toss a handful of sand in to
make it fizz). A boat trip across the Waikato River to the silica
terraces at **Orakei Korako** reveals one of New Zealand's best
thermal areas, much less visited because of its remoteness.
Some evening tours include a swim in a hot pool. To the east
lies vast Kaingaroa State Forest, much of it planted with fast-
growing radiata pine during the Depression of the 1930s.

At **Huka Falls,** 4 km (2.5 miles) south on the road to
Taupo, the Waikato River leaps a ledge and plunges into a
churning maelstrom. View it from the bridge spanning the
river or take a jet-boat ride for awesome views of the falls
from their base. Craters of the Moon (almost opposite) is a
thermal area that sprang into life in the 1950s when geothermal power generation lowered underground water levels.

Taupo

The region around Taupo, long synonymous with angling, is
now gaining a reputation with golfers. The golfing connection comes from Wairakei International, one of the country's
finest courses. NZ$2.5 million was spent to improve it fur-
ther with the addition of 31 bunkers.

New Zealand's largest lake, **Lake Taupo** covers 616 sq km
(382.6 sq miles) and gives rise to the country's longest river, the

Waikato (354 km/220 miles). Taupo's waters yield about 700 tons of trout a year. As it is illegal to buy and sell trout, the only way to sample the fish is to catch it yourself. Summer is a good time to catch trout (they are fat from feasting on green beetles), but dedicated anglers prefer the spawning season in autumn and winter. June to September is best for rainbow trout. No angler can call himself complete if he hasn't cast a fly into the **Tongariro River**, known to fishing enthusiasts worldwide. Taupo Visitor Center on Tongariro Street (Tel: 07/ 376-0027; www.laketauponz.com) can advise on fishing and licenses, and even on helicopter transport to super-secluded bush-land streams and pools. If you tire of fishing, Taupo offers swimming, water-skiing, boating, and a few more offbeat attractions as well, such as bungee-jumping at a scenic spot on the Waikato River. You can leap from a platform jutting over a cliff or—even better—watch others do it!

You can visit Cherry Island, a low-key wildlife park, opt for the fairly easy two-hour walk to the top of Mt. Tauhara, or try some barbecued prawns at **Taupo Prawn Park**. It's always roundup time at the prawn park; giant freshwater prawns are raised in geothermally heated water.

Tongariro National Park

Tongariro National Park, a World Heritage site a short drive south of Taupo, is worth a scenic flight. It straddles the junction of two of the earth's tectonic plates, causing friction that forces steam and hot springs to the earth's surface. Three great volcanic peaks, considered guardian deities by the Maoris, dominate the park. The region's paramount Maori chief presented the three mountains—Mt. Tongariro, Mt. Ngauruhoe, and Mt. Ruapehu—to the nation in 1887 in an act of generous confidence, creating New Zealand's first national park. Mt. Tongariro's northern circuit is one of the country's great walks.

*In Tongariro National Park, magnificent Mt. Ngauruhoe is
one of three volcanic peaks that are sacred to the Maoris.*

Mt. Ngauruhoe is a conical, single-vent volcano. **Mt. Ruapehu** is the site of the country's largest ski area. The summit
erupted in 1996, blasting such an amount of volcanic ash and
steam into the air that warnings were issued to passenger aircraft not to fly too close. Despite a bold "go ski a volcano"
campaign after the rumblings died down, the North Island ski
season was disastrous that year. Mt. Ruapehu has now gone
quiet, and its ski resorts of **Whakapapa** and **Turoa** offer huge
expanses of varied terrain and attract about 400,000 skiers and
snowboarders a year. The resorts' high altitude makes for long-
lasting snow; even summer skiing is sometimes possible.
Hunting permits are available. Whakapapa Visitor Center (Tel:
07/ 892-3729) has details.

East Cape and Hawke's Bay
Gloriously sunny and very beautiful in parts, this area is less
familiar to overseas visitors, although the Pacific Coast High-

way around the East Cape to Gisborne may change that. **Gisborne** is the first town in the world to behold the new day, because of its proximity to the International Date Line. New Zealand opera diva Dame Kiri Te Kanawa performed there to greet the new millennium.

Hawke's Bay province, the "fruit bowl of New Zealand," is also one of the country's prime wine-producing regions. The sunny climate and low humidity are perfect for late-maturing grape varieties such as Cabernet Sauvignon and Chardonnay. Mission Vineyards, managed by the Brothers of the Society of Mary, is a good place to start the Hawke's Bay wine trail. Gisborne's winemakers excel at Chardonnay, which varies in flavor from the American variety.

The twin cities of Napier and Hastings engage in friendly rivalry for the title of the leading Hawke's Bay town. In 1931 the district suffered a disastrous earthquake. Both cities were reduced to rubble and Napier was swept by fire. Some 4,000 hectares of seabed were raised in the quake.

Napier was rebuilt in the lively, angular, and streamlined Art-Deco style in vogue at the time. The best way to appreciate the buildings is to join a guided walk with the Art Deco Trust (2pm daily during the summer, less frequently at other times).

Don't miss the gannet sanctuary at **Cape Kidnappers**: drive the 21 km (13 miles) to Clifton Domain, then walk the remaining 8 km (5 miles). Coach tours are available. Summer is the time to see some 4,500 pairs of golden crowned gannets and their downy chicks. Adult birds have snowy plumage, distinctive yellow heads, and strong black-tipped pinions.

Mt. Taranaki

Lone, conical-shaped Mt. Taranaki—known as New Zealand's Mt. Fuji and popular with Japanese tourists—is a snow-capped, dormant volcano. The summit rises 2,518 m

(8,260 ft) from bright green farmland, its lower slopes thickly forested. The mountain offers good skiing, and you can climb it in a day. But don't attempt the full ascent without a guide; in spite of its beauty, the mountain can be treacherous.

Mt. Taranaki serves as a dramatic backdrop for the town of **New Plymouth.** Take a daytime stroll to view the gardens of **Pukekura Park,** one of the finest in the country; then perhaps visit again at night to see the floodlit waterfall.

Further botanical delights wait at the **Pukeiti Rhododendron Trust,** 29 km (18 miles) out of town on the Upper Carrington Road, where 10,000 rhododendrons flourish. Five hundred of the world's 800 known species grow here.

If you are heading south when you leave New Plymouth, stop at cheese factories in Eltham or Stratford if you want to sample the French-style cheese for which the area is gaining a reputation.

Wanganui

To confuse spellers, the town of Wanganui lies at the mouth of the Whanganui River. (An 'h' was inserted into the spelling of the river, reverting to the preferred Maori version

Outwit Those Sandflies!

You don't have to worry about venomous creepy-crawlies in New Zealand. The only poisonous spider, the katipo, is rare and retiring. Bites from it are so uncommon they are reported in newspapers when they occur. And New Zealand has no snakes. But there is a flying pest known to the local Maoris as *te namu namu*, the biting sandfly. These little insects, tireless and insatiable, can't fly fast enough to catch you when you're walking. They strike when you stop for a rest—unless you have armed yourself with insect repellent. According to Maori legend, sandflies were created by Hinenui-tepo, goddess of the underworld.

of the word, but the town prefers to be spelled without an 'h'.)
Wanganui displays in its museum awesome skeletons of moas,
the giant birds hunted to extinction in pre-European times. Ascend the Durie Hill elevator for a splendid view of the town.
Putiki Church (1937) contains memorable Maori carvings. Try
one of the jet-boat tours on the Whanganui River, which often
include a bush walk to the Bridge to Nowhere, which disappears into lush undergrowth. A most unorthodox attraction on
the Whanganui River is **The Flying Fox,** offering unique accommodation and a boutique brewery where you can sample
manuka beer (made from tea tree leaves). It's located 14 minutes from Wanganui and can be accessed only by an aerial
cable-way or boat. www.theflyingfox.co.nz.

WELLINGTON

Wellington possesses an assurance and an international flair
that comes with being the country's artistic and cultural capital as well as its capital city. With a regional population of
about 440,000, including about 200,000 in the city itself,
Wellington is considerably smaller than its northern rival,
Auckland, which it replaced as capital in 1865.

Just 20 years ago, Wellington was a quiet place where crit-
ics claimed you could fire a cannon down the main street at
midnight on Saturday without risk of hitting anyone. Since
then, New Zealand's capital has blossomed into a vibrant,
urban destination with a lively nightlife. The city's charm de-
rives partly from its quirky topography, with wooden, turn-of-
the century houses clinging to steep hillsides bristling with
native bush and clumps of arum lilies. Zig-zag streets spill
downwards to the heart of the city, the harbor, and the affluent

*From rugged hills to soaring skyscrapers, Wellington
reveals a marriage of city flair and natural charm.*

Creatures from the deep on exhibit at Te Papa Museum.

promenade of Oriental Bay. The layout reminds some visitors of San Francisco.

Wellington is nicknamed the "Windy City" and that's no exaggeration; it's usually breezy and at times the wind can knock you clean off your feet. In the business district, old higgledy-piggledy Wellington has virtually been replaced by soaring modern buildings—a cause of regret for many who loved the haphazard character of the place. Wellington boasts a thriving café culture and some 450 restaurants—pick up a *Wine and Food Guide* from the Visitor Information Center in Civic Square (Tel: 04/801-4000). The center also has details of sightseeing tours that will take you to Wellington's historic landmarks and views. Walking around the major points of interest on your own takes about four hours.

 Civic Square, near the Visitor Center, is a good place to start. Here you will find the City Gallery (a contemporary art gallery), the refurbished Town Hall, the Performing Arts Center, and the City Library, with its unusual metal palm tree pillars. A striking bridge, decorated with wooden and steel sculptures, links the square with the waterfront. All these eclectic elements blend into a striking and harmonious whole—no small achievement.

Not far away stands the monolithic rectangular bulk of **Te Papa, Museum of New Zealand.** It may not be the most inspiring structure from the outside, but inside, this museum is so revolutionary it has developed into a major tourist attraction. *Te Papa* ("Our Place" in Maori) uses thrilling, interactive technology to involve visitors in the action. A motion simulator conveys visitors back to prehistoric native bush in the days before humans had arrived in *Aotearoa*. An attraction called Time Warp, one of Te Papa's most popular, includes a simulated view of a volcanic eruption. www. tepapa.govt.nz

Through simulation technology, you can ride a wind-surfer or a whale, shear a sheep, or take a bungee-jump. You can experience a simulated earthquake, see the eruptions of Mt. Ruapehu, and learn the stories of New Zealand's natural disasters. Maori culture is presented graphically—there's a *marae,* or village, on the premises—and the hands-on activity areas are so popular with children they have to be dragged away.

Wellington's main commercial street, **Lambton Quay**, used to run along the waterfront, but reclamation has pushed the land out. A plaque in the pavement at Stewart Dawson's Corner marks the old shoreline. New buildings in Wellington are specially strengthened to handle earthquakes. Take the **funicular** (from Cable Car Lane, opposite Grey Street) up to **Kelburn** to enjoy the views of the inner harbor and central city. Paths to the right of the terminal lead to the Lady Norwood Rose Garden and Begonia House.

The National Library building on Molesworth Street is the home of the **Alexander Turnbull Library,** with its fine collection of books, manuscripts, photographs, and paintings relating to New Zealand. The exhibition gallery is well worth a visit. Weekdays you can join a tour of the building.

Three buildings make up the **Parliament** complex (entrance on Molesworth St.): an austere main building (1922), a neo-

Gothic General Assembly Library complete with arches and spires (1897), and an impressive domed structure known as "the Beehive." In front of the complex stands a lofty statue of the much-loved prime minister Richard John Seddon, whose proudest claim was "I am a humanist." Tours of the Library and main building take place when parliament is not sitting.

Nearby **St. Paul's Cathedral**, in pink concrete, recalls the Spanish Colonial architectural style of San Diego's Balboa Park. **Old Government Building** (1876) at the north end of Lambton Quay is the world's second largest wooden building, constructed almost entirely of native timber. The cost so vastly exceeded estimates that the government decided to give it no official inauguration, in the hope no one would notice the cost.

Marine Drive, which starts at Oriental Bay, presents a wide variety of coastline, from the sand beaches of chic suburbia to jagged rocks and gray, rolling sea. At **Oriental Bay** itself, make a detour to the Mt. Victoria lookout (sign-posted), for superb city and harbor views—and astonishing gusts of wind at times! The stone memorial commemorates the American Antarctic explorer Rear Admiral Byrd (1887–1957), who made New Zealand the starting point for his expeditions and achieved the first flight over the South Pole.

For refreshment, The Malthouse, an historic pub on Willis Street, offers one of the world's largest selections of naturally fermented beers on draft. Courtenay Place is lined with bars, clubs, and trendy eateries, and nearby Cuba Street has plenty of nightlife options. One of the best swimming beaches is Days Bay, a 30-minute ferry ride across the harbor.

NELSON and MARLBOROUGH

Three waterways, Queen Charlotte Sound, Pelorus Sound, and Kenepuru Sound, penetrate the northernmost part of the South Island. They form an immense marine playground of pristine beaches and secluded coves, many accessible only by boat. The Interislander ferries crossing Cook Strait pass close to **The Brothers,** a group of barren islands inhabited by the rare tuatara, only surviving member of the "beak-headed" reptile family that became extinct over 100 million years ago. Dolphins (including the small, rare Hectors dolphin found only off New Zealand) often ride the ship's bow wave. Dolphins are better suited than humans to Cook Strait, which can be quite smooth or very rough indeed, depending on your luck!

Eventually the ferry turns into Tory Channel and continues up Queen Charlotte Sound to the deep-water port of **Picton.** Picton's sights include the Community Museum, with relics of the harsh old whaling days, and two venerable sailing ships moored close to the town: the *Echo* (beached in Picton Harbour), the last sail trading vessel in New Zealand; and the *Edwin Fox* (in Shakespeare Bay), one of the oldest sailing ships in existence, built as a tea clipper in 1843. In the Crimean War it carried renowned English nurse Florence Nightingale.

Marlborough Sounds

The Sounds are best explored by boat. Picton offers an astonishing variety of vessels for hire, from charter launches to water taxis. Day cruises are an easy option; kayaking is ewarding and fun. Historic spots in the Sounds include Ship Cove, visited five times by Captain Cook, Motuara Island, where Cook raised the British flag, and French Pass, navigated in colonial times by the Frenchman Dumont d'Urville, who gave his name to the large island lying offshore. If you're reasonably fit you can trek the whole 67 km (41.5 miles) from Ship Cove to Anakawa over four days along Queen Charlotte Walkway, overnighting at campsites and in private lodges such as Furneaux Lodge, The Portage, and Te Punga.

John Guard's whaling station on **Te Awaiti Bay** (Tory Channel), founded in 1827, is said to have been the first European settlement on the South Island, and John's wife the first white woman to live there.

The main water tours pass through Queen Charlotte's Grove Arm to **Double Cove,** where tame snapper are fed twice daily. The Queen Charlotte Sound mail run varies its route day to day, and the Pelorus Sound jaunt sets off four times a week from Havelock, at the head of Pelorus Sound. For outstanding fishing, you can arrange to be dropped off and picked up again later in the day; Pelorus and Kenepuru sounds are recommended. In addition to the snapper, blue and red cod, terakihi, tuna, kahawai (sea trout), grouper (hapuka), garfish, and butterfish proliferate.

The coastal township of **Kaikoura,** about halfway between Blenheim and Christchurch, is still a whaling town, in a kinder sense. Whales are no longer hunted, but the giant mammals can be viewed year round and local tour operators boast a 95% success rate in locating them for visitors who venture out to sea. You can spend a magical afternoon watching magnificent sperm whales—or don flippers and snorkel to join the dolphins in their watery world. Mincke, humpback, and the southern right whale can also be sighted. Crayfish abound (they're delicious and can be bought ready-boiled from nearby shacks). The name Kaikoura means "meal of crayfish."

Blenheim, 29 km (18 miles) south of Picton, claims to be the sunniest spot in New Zealand. It hosts the New Zealand Food and Wine Festival the second Saturday of February each year. Regional wineries are open seven days a week year-round. Many lie within cycling distance of Blenheim, for those who fancy pedaling. Marlborough, more than any other region, has placed New Zealand's wines on the world

Ocean majesty: what better way to see the sun go down than on a whale watch?

map. The region is home to more than 30 wineries, including Montana and the renowned Cloudy Bay.

Nelson City and Environs

Beaches, sunshine, spectacular sunsets, and a thriving arts scene attract visitors to **Nelson** (population 43,000). The region has the most sunshine of any place in New Zealand—over 2500 hours annually. Situated on Tasman Bay, the small city of Nelson has become a haven for artists and craftspeople. Local clay is prized for pottery and more than 70 full-time potters work in the area. Painters, glass blowers, and jewelers, plus a thriving café culture, give the city an arty feel.

Christ Church Cathedral, set in pleasantly landscaped grounds, dominates urban views. Nelson's other main building (much less attractive) is a modern council complex at the end of Trafalgar Street, notable only for its peculiar, bluntly truncated tower. The Suter Art Gallery at 208 Bridge Street (not far

A Maori artisan from Fayne Robinson Arts and Crafts displays his handiwork.

from Trafalgar Street; www.thesuter.org.nz), is one of the South Island's finest galleries; watercolors predominate but plenty of scope is given to ceramics and local potters. The small Nelson Provincial Museum at Isel Park, 6 km (3.7 miles) south of Nelson, boasts an extensive photographic collection. Picturesque Isel House is open nearby. Several colonial houses in South Street have been turned into galleries, featuring contemporary pottery fashioned from local clay. For a view over the whole city and Tasman Bay, climb Botanical Hill. You look down on the playing field where the country's first rugby match took place in 1870—a momentous date in Kiwi history. Nelson's best beach, the golden stretch of Tahunanui, lies 5 km (3.1 miles) from the town center (there are some pleasant seafood eateries on the way). Nelson is well known for its annual Wearable Arts Awards. Held every September, this fashion extravaganza features weird and wonderful designs by national and international designers, craftspeople and artists (www.worldof wearableart.com).

In addition to the arts, Nelson is known for its national parks and walking trails. Three national parks lie within 90 minutes of the city: Nelson Lakes alpine park, wilderness Kahurangi, and coastal Abel Tasman National Park. Kahurangi and Abel Tasman feature major multi-day walking tracks. The Heaphy Track traverses Kahurangi National Park to the West Coast. Or you can explore the 57,000 hectares of Nelson Lakes National Park. Most tracks can be walked all year round. Picnic spots around Lakes Rotoiti and Rotoroa are surrounded by red, silver, and black beech forests and are rich in rare plants. **Abel Tasman National Park,** to the northwest, offers opportunities for camping, boating, swimming, and hiking. To reach the main point of entry, you pass through the fruit-growing district of Motueka and take the road leading to Takaka.

On the wine front, Pinot Noir is challenging Chardonnay these days; and Sauvignon Blancs and Rieslings from this region have also garnered national and international awards. Many wineries have tasting rooms and restaurants and children's amusements. The Nelson region is the only area in New Zealand that grows hops for the making of beer. Boutique breweries hereabouts include McCashin's Brewery and Malthouse (Mac's beers are a national favorite and a "Black Mac" is well worth sampling) and Harrington's Brewery.

SOUTH ISLAND'S WEST COAST

The wild West Coast of the South Island occupies a special place in the New Zealand psyche. Rugged individualists, eccentrics, and wild tales abound. The coast itself is a narrow strip of land wedged between the Tasman Sea and the Southern Alps. No more than 50 km (31.5 miles) wide at any point, the West Coast spans glaciers, lush forests, and soaring mountain peaks. Few places so narrow have the power to evoke the Swiss Alps, the American Rockies, and even parts of Alaska (depending on which part you tour). Gold, coal, timber, and greenstone run through stories of rivalry between Irish and

Museums and Attractions

Auckland Museum, *The Domain, Auckland; Tel: (09) 309-0443.* Geology and seismology of New Zealand, plus excellent Maori exhibits in the Maoritanga room. Open daily 10am–5pm. Admission free (donations encouraged), fees for special exhibitions; www.akmuseum.co.nz. (See page 30)

The Sky Tower, *Federal and Victoria Streets, Auckland.* Higher than the Eiffel Tower and at 328 meters (1,076 feet) New Zealand's highest structure, this gives superb views of Auckland and harbors. Open daily 8:30am–midnight. Admission: NZ$15 plus NZ$3 for upper observation deck; www.skycity.co.nz. (See page 28)

Auckland Art Gallery, *Auckland; Tel: (09) 307-7700.* The Heritage Gallery (Wellesley and Kitchener Streets) concentrates on traditional New Zealand art. Admission free. The New Gallery (Wellesley and Lorne streets) looks at modern contributions, with interesting fusions of Maori and pakeha culture. Admission: NZ$4. Both open daily 10am–5pm. (See page 30)

Kelly Tarlton's Antarctic Encounter and Underwater World, *23 Tamaki Dr., Orakei, Auckland; Tel: (09) 528-0603.* Aquarium housed in old storm-water tanks allows you to walk under the sea in a clear tunnel. Antarctic display comes complete with live King Penguins. Sharks are fed at 2pm on Tue, and Thur*. Admission: NZ$25. Open daily summer 9am–8pm; winter 9am–6pm; www.kellytarltonstours.co.nz. (See page 31)

Museum Of Transport and Technology (MOTAT), *Great North Rd., Western Springs, Auckland; Tel: (09) 846-7020; www.aucklandcity.govt.nz* Look for the exhibition about South Island farmer and inventor Richard Pearse, who may have made a powered flight before the Wright Brothers. Admission: NZ$10. Open daily 10am–5pm. (See page 31)

Te Papa (Museum of New Zealand), *Cable Street, Wellington; Tel: (04) 381-7000.* New Zealand's past, present, and future through advanced interactive technology. Admission free; fees for special exhibitions. Open daily 10am–6pm (to 9pm on Thur) www.tepapa.govt.nz. (See page 55)

Katherine Mansfield Birthplace, *25 Tinakori Road, Wellington; Tel: (04) 473-7268.* Birthplace of New Zealand's most famous short story writer. Mansfield spent five years here and mentioned it in a couple of stories. Admission NZ$5.50. Open daily 10am–4pm (closes 2:30pm on Mon).

Christchurch Cathedral, *Cathedral Square, Christchurch; Tel: (03) 366-0046.* Panoramic views can be enjoyed from the spire of this Gothic revival edifice, consecrated in 1881. Admission to spire: NZ$4. Open weekdays 8:30am–8pm, Sat 9am–5pm, Sun 7:30am–8pm; www.library.christchurch.org.nz. (See page 65)

Canterbury Museum, *Rolleston Ave., Christchurch; Tel: (03) 366-5000.* Exploration of Antarctica, the early colonization of Canterbury, and geological exhibits. Suggested admission: NZ$5. Open daily 9am–5pm; www.artists.co.nz. (See page 66)

International Antarctic Centre, *Orchard Rd., Christchurch Airport; Tel: (03) 358-9896.* The closest you can get to experiencing the snow and ice of Antarctica without going there and freezing. Built as a base for the US and New Zealand Antarctic programs. Admission: NZ$18. Open daily Oct–Mar 9am–8pm, April–Sept 9am–5:30pm; www.iceberg.co.nz.

Otago Museum, *419 Great King St., Dunedin, Tek, (03) 474-7474.* Well-presented and thought provoking displays on natural history and Maori and Pacific Islands anthropology. Donations requested; Discovery World hands-on science exhibition: NZ$6. Open daily 10am–5pm, Sat and Sun 1pm–5pm; www.otagomuseum.govt.nz. (See page 80)

Larnach's Castle, *Pukehiki, Dunedin; Tel: (03) 476-1616.* This lavish Victorian folly of mixed architectural styles, designed at stupendous expense by a deranged merchant politician, is Dunedin's best-known building. Admission: NZ$12. Open daily 9am–5pm; www.larnachcastle.co.nz. (See page 81).

Scottish immigrants, set against a background of shantytowns, strong-willed women, and quietly spoken, hard-hitting men. The West Coast is still strewn with old machinery, tunnels, water races, and the creaking remnants of ghost towns.

In the days when pubs were required to close their doors at 6pm (this archaic law remained in force for 50 years until 1967), West Coasters simply smiled and kept on drinking their beer. Sealers were the first Europeans to settle these parts; gold miners descended after the yellow metal was discovered in the 1850s. Isolated, irrepressible, and individualistic, West Coasters add a touch of irony and humor to the South Island scene.

The northern West Coast has become an adventure holiday destination, offering rafting and caving, jet-boating and grand treks. Full- and half-day nature and wilderness tours are available. Five days can be spent traveling the whole West Coast Road, but shorter sections of the road can be traversed in less time. Impressive scenery enlivens the drive from Inangahua Junction to Westport, through the Lower Buller Gorge. You can visit many of the coal towns, including the ghost settlement of Denniston and Granity, where enormous oval boulders and a scattering of gemstones litter the beach. Punakaiki boasts "pancake rocks" (limestone formations like giant flapjacks) and surf blowholes. The coast is famous for its whitebait, tiny fish that swim in shoals and are netted in rivers. (The whitebait season runs from September to November).

Greymouth, locally known as "Grey," is the largest coastal town, terminus of the TranzAlpine train and location of the replica gold mining town, Shantytown, which is a bit touristy but quite fun, complete with jail and gallows.

Hokitika (population 4,000) was probably more interesting when it was "capital of the gold-fields." Today it's the greenstone capital. You can visit greenstone factories and watch craftsmen cut and polish this durable, attractive variety of jade.

The West Coast Historical Museum has an audio-visual display every 30 minutes. The town is also home to the infamous Hokitika Wild Food Festival, held the second weekend of March, when all sorts of weird and wonderful food is served.

Okarito, first point in New Zealand to be spied by European eyes (those of Abel Tasman and his crew) is now the site of a small hamlet used as a setting by author Keri Hulme for her Booker Prize-winning novel *The Bone People*. Okarito Lagoon can be visited by kayak. If you're lucky, you may glimpse the white heron (*Egretta alba*), celebrated in Maori legend for its snowy plumage and graceful flight. The bird is rare in New Zealand and if you see one in your lifetime, you're fortunate.

CHRISTCHURCH

Christchurch (population about 330,000) has been called "the most English city outside England" so often that the term has become a cliché. Yet the comparison is inescapable. Some visitors claim that Christchurch is now more English than England itself, having failed to incorporate changes made in Britain over the past 50 years. Conceived as an outpost of Anglicanism and laid out on the lines of an English university town around a cathedral, Christchurch was planned as a haven of quiet gardens and calm, orderly ways. The first settlers (called the Canterbury Pilgrims after the province in which Christchurch is situated) disembarked in Lyttelton Harbour in 1850. They had been specially selected by their hometown ministers, who were urged to ensure that all the pilgrims be sober, industrious, honest—and under 40. Inland, on a plain in the Canterbury district, they found their town ready planned and endowed with nostalgic street names.

Christchurch rapidly became center of a prosperous farming region. By the mid-1860s a million sheep grazed in Canterbury pastures. Today Canterbury lamb is extensively exported and the area rates as the country's chief grain producer. At the heart of the grid system on which central Christchurch is built stands **Christchurch Cathedral,** built in early English Gothic style out of local stone. Marble tablets near the Post Office are inscribed with the names of the Canterbury Pilgrims. Victoria Square sports a staid statue of the eponymous queen and another of Captain Cook. The Town Hall, opened in 1972, overlooks the Avon River (another British touch).

Over 3,000 hectares of parks and playing fields lie within Christchurch boundaries. The Botanical Gardens are tucked into a loop of the Avon, adjacent to expansive **Hagley Park,** planted entirely in deciduous trees from the Northern Hemisphere and astonishingly lovely in spring and fall. Many private gardens are open all year and guided walking tours cover the most beautiful (and sometimes otherwise restricted) areas. The Christchurch-Canterbury Visitor Center, in the Old Post Office building in Cathedral Square (Tel: 03/379-9629) has details of these tours. An easy way to introduce yourself to Christchurch is to take a ride on the restored historic tram that circles the inner city, conveying passengers from the Square to the shops and galleries of the Arts Center and the pastel-hued Georgian cafés and houses of New Regent Street.

Much of the city has been pedestrianized, which makes for easy wandering. Its flat topography makes it perfect for cycling, and bikes can be easily hired. A walk along Gloucester Street and then down Rolleston Avenue brings you to the Botanical Gardens area of Hagley Park and to Canterbury Museum, another Mountfort building (1870), where the Exploration of Antarctica hall vividly illustrates Christchurch's association with Antarctic exploration. The adjacent Mc-

England, England! Weeping willows, straw boaters, rowboats...the Avon River captures the essence of Christchurch.

Dougall Art Gallery displays two Rodin sculptures. At nearby Christ's College—run on the lines of a traditional British "public" (i.e., private) school—the boys still wear straw boaters. Christchurch Arts Center, farther down Rolleston Avenue in the former Canterbury University buildings, boasts galleries, a cinema, theater, craft workshop, and pottery center. You can visit the cramped basement laboratory where nuclear physicist Ernest Rutherford, the first man to split the atom, studied before transferring to Cambridge University in England. Other Christchurch attractions include New Zealand's first casino (since eclipsed by Auckland's big new Sky Tower complex), the Royal New Zealand Air Force Museum, and the sound-and-light show at the International Antarctic Center.

South of the city rise the **Port Hills.** The Mt. Cavendish Gondola and the Summit Road Drive along the crest of the hills afford splendid views of the Canterbury Plains, with the Southern Alps to the west and Lyttelton Harbour to the east. En route you encounter the **Sign of the Takahe,** an elaborate tearoom resembling a Tudor hall, complete with carvings, coats of arms, and heraldic shields. For a scenic ride to remember, take the TranzAlpine Express through the Alps to Greymouth, or the Trans Coastal along the Kaikoura coast to Picton.

Akaroa

Some 82 km (51 miles) from Christchurch on the southern side of Banks Peninsula lies the tiny settlement of Akaroa, settled by French colonists. Family names and street names reflect the town's beginnings as a supply station for French whalers—you can stroll along Rue Viard, Rue Lavaud, and Rue Croix. This picturesque little hamlet resembles a quaint English seaside town more than a French village, but souvenirs of its Gallic origins are cherished: the willows are said to have grown from cuttings transported from Napoleon's grave, old vineyards survive in places, and ancient fruit trees fill the air with scents as sweet as any found in a Normandy orchard. On the foreshore a stone marks the place where the French landed. Nearby are trypots, vessels used for rendering whale blubber, and the Customs House. Evocative exhibits are on display at Langlois-Eteveneaux House and Museum.

MT. COOK NATIONAL PARK

The five-hour drive from Christchurch to Mt. Cook National Park traverses some of New Zealand's most scenic landscapes. Lakes and golden, tussock-covered hills give way to the Southern Alps, a world of cloud and ice, glacier, and rock, mountain streams and alpine flowers. One mountain towers above the rest—cloud piercing Mt. Cook, New Zealand's highest mountain at 3,754 m (12,315 ft).

Surrounding Mt. Cook, or Aorangi ("Cloud-Piercer") to the Maoris, are 22 of the 27 New Zealand peaks with altitudes of 3,000 m (9,840 ft) or more. Mt. Cook was first scaled on Christmas Day, 1894. New Zealander Sir Edmund Hillary, first conqueror of Mt. Everest, is one of many mountaineers to have completed the climb. Only in 1970 was Mt. Cook's most difficult face, the Caroline, scaled.

Glacial ice was the prime sculptor of the Southern Alps. Most famous of the region's many glaciers is the Tasman, 29 km (18 miles) in length and up to 3 km (1.8 miles) wide, one of the longest outside polar regions and the Himalayas. One of the Tasman's subsidiaries, the Hochstetter, ends in a 1,000-m (3,280-ft) descent so tortuous and chaotic that it is known as an "icefall."

Skiing in New Zealand started around here, when three men shod themselves with elements of farm machinery to cross the area known as the Grand Plateau. The year was 1893. Foreign-made skis were introduced in 1909, but it was only after World War I that skiing grew in popularity. Today you can fly to the head of the Tasman Glacier for the ski experience of a lifetime, gliding 13 km (8 miles) down the snow-covered ice river (experienced skiers only).

Glacial Majesty

Franz Josef and Fox are the most accessible and largest of 60 glaciers in Mt. Cook National Park. They rank among the scenic glories of New Zealand. Opinions vary as to which is more impressive, but the question fades when you stand confronted by the glittering majesty of these massive white-and-turquoise ice rivers thrusting into subtropical bushland. Both flow down from the snow-fields of the Alps to within a surprisingly short distance of the sea. Most glaciers around the world are in retreat as global warming continues, but these two are still advancing, following a recent series of cold winters. In no other mild climates do glaciers descend to so close to the surf.

Glacier walks are conducted regularly, graded to suit various levels of fitness. The weather can change abruptly, so dress accordingly. Wear appropriate footwear and don't try solitary strolls. Always inform someone of your intention if you decide to go on a lengthy hike. Guides are available and necessary. All equipment, including boots and socks, is provided on guided trips. When the weather permits, scenic ski-plane and helicopter flights are worth the expense.

The **Franz Josef Glacier** was first sighted by Captain Cook as he sailed along the coast in 1769. The glacier was 3 km (1.8 miles) closer to the sea in those days. Geologist Julius von Haast named the glacier in 1862 after the emperor of his native Austria. Today's Franz Josef is a mere 7,000 years old, but it had an even grander parent—which reached right to the coast. Today's glacier descends some 2,280 m (1,416 ft), terminating in a spectacular icefall that feeds the Waiho River, whose name, "Smoking Water," was inspired by the vapor rising from its surface. The river actually begins under the ice.

A Glacier Valley Walk (one hour round-trip) starts at the end of the Franz Josef Glacier access road, following the Waiho River to the glacier terminal. Check track conditions before departure and heed all signs. Many other walks are available, including the one-hour round-trip Douglas Walk, which starts with 4 km (2.5 miles) along the glacier access road, then a five-minute bushwalk to Peters Pool for reflective views of the glacier, then through forest to exit 500 m (1,640 ft) down the road from the starting point. For a scene of sublime mountain grandeur (and a truly awesome altar backdrop), gaze through the chancel window of St. James Anglican Church (1931).

Cone Rock and Chalet Lookout provide spectacular views of **Fox Glacier.** Mirror-like Lake Matheson catches chocolate-box reflections of snowy peaks and bush-covered hills. One of the best walks skirts the lake and takes an hour. You'll be cheered by the sound of chiming bellbirds and accompanied by fantails. The walk to Lake Gault offers even more varied bird life. Very early morning is the best time. As for the glaciers themselves, try to view them at sunset, when the high peaks glow like opals and the lower reaches withdraw into violet shadow.

With Mt. Cook Village and the most famous hotel in New Zealand, the **Hermitage,** in the vicinity, this alpine area offers activities all the year round. Walking tops the list. Head out along Bowen Track to Hooker Valley, a good place to view Mt. Cook. Or try the route to Kea Point, which passes through sub-alpine scrub and across moraine to a point overlooking Mueller Glacier, with the dizzy grandeur of Mt. Sefton above.

Among birds, you'll see the rock wren, the grey warbler, the tiny rifleman, and the plump native pigeon. You'll hear moreporks (the native owl) calling at night and will be amused—and possibly peeved—by the antics of the kea (*Nestor notabilis*), a mountain parrot that looks drab green until it reveals brilliant scarlet under its wings. Keas are the most mischievous ragamuffins you're likely to meet. They steal food, toboggan down roofs, hang around campsites, ransack backpacks for sandwiches, and gleefully rip to pieces anything you leave around, all the time keeping an impudent eye on you. Alpine flowers include the mountain buttercup or Mt. Cook lily, which blooms from November to January. The Visitor Center distributes excellent brochures on the region's flora and fauna and advises on activities in the area.

☛ QUEENSTOWN

Queenstown, in a bay on the shores of **Lake Wakatipu,** occupies one of the world's most dramatically scenic spots. It was only a matter of time before the world discovered it. Queenstown has become probably the most visited spot in the South Island, offering the attractions of lake and mountain (there's top-class skiing nearby at Coronet Peak), plus a year-round party atmosphere.

International flights head directly into Queenstown from Australia without stopping at Christchurch. In winter, skiers and snow-boarders hit the slopes. In summer, trekkers set off on some of New Zealand's most famous alpine treks, such as the rugged wilderness of Mt. Aspiring and Fiordland national parks.

Queenstown offers plenty of lakeside hotels, over 100 restaurants, and no end of bars. More venerable local landmarks include the town's stone library (1877) and St. Peter's Anglican Church. The Skyline Gondola zips up **Bob's Peak** (446 m-/1,463 ft) in four minutes for the best views of the town and the lake. The Skyline Café at the top is reasonably priced. You can paraglide to the bottom or descend more sedately.

Active romantics leave Queenstown at midnight to climb 1,764-m (5,786-ft) Ben Lomond so that they'll reach the summit in time to watch the sun rise over **The Remarkables.** If you contemplate this, let someone know you're going. Allow a full day to ascend the 2,342-m (7,682 ft) Remarkables themselves.

The **TSS *Earnslaw*,** a picturesque old twin-screw, coal-burning steamer with a tall smokestack, is featured in many postcard views of Lake Wakatipu. The Earnslaw may be getting on, but she has young ideas: lunchtime champagne cruises, poetry readings, and evening dinner dances. The boat has enjoyed a resurgence of popularity since the movie *Titanic* was released. The two vessels are

And some prefer their scenery upside down...Bungee-jumping off Kawarau Bridge.

of a similar vintage—the *Earnslaw* was launched in 1912, the year the *Titanic* went down. But don't worry—the *Earnslaw's* skipper keeps a keen eye out for icebergs.

Launches (less picturesque than the *Earnslaw,* but faster) cross the lake to big sheep stations like Cecil Peak or Walter Peak, where you can watch a sheep-dog display, meet the animals, or just enjoy afternoon tea.

Sun worship: a baby seal warms up on a rock in a Kaikoura seal colony.

For relaxation, you can fish Lake Wakatipu for rainbow and brown trout and quinnat salmon. Want something more exhilarating? Try bungee-jumping at the site where the pastime began, A. J. Hackett's leaping point atop the 43-m **Kawarau Suspension Bridge.** The company has another site at Skippers Canyon Bridge. www.ajhackett.com. On wild Shotover River you can go jet-boating, whitewater rafting, bungee-jumping, or helicopter flightseeing. Jet-boat trips move so fast, the scenery blurs. Raft trips on the river are another option.

About 23 km (14.3 miles) from Queenstown, the former mining center of **Arrowtown** retains a charm despite the tourist buses and day-trippers. The town is enchanting in summer, a dream of smoky amber and bright gold in fall, as the old trees change color and the air is crisp with early frost. Wood and stone cottages, the homes of miners long gone, border the main street. It's best appreciated after the tour buses depart.

If you didn't miss a heartbeat jet-boating, then test yourself on **Skippers Canyon.** Here, not far from the bungee-jump site, guided tours traverse a narrow, stony road edged by precipitous drops. Huge amounts of gold came out of Skippers. The wild roses that bloom all around were planted by the miners to provide rosehip syrup to supplement their scanty diet and prevent scurvy.

Queenstown is the start-point of two of New Zealand's best guided hikes—the Routeburn and the Hollyford Valley Walk, majestic routes through bush and alpine landscape. If you drive from Queenstown to Te Anau, you'll pass the town of Kingston. In summer a gleaming black restored 1915 steam locomotive, the *Kingston Flyer,* proudly puffs its way from here to the tiny settlement of Fairlight.

FIORDLAND

A hauntingly beautiful world of wild valleys, soaring mountains, and startlingly blue water—that's **Fiordland National Park,** New Zealand's biggest and most spectacular. The region remains sparsely populated and, in parts, virtually unexplored. Thriving fur-seal colonies attracted some of the earliest European settlers here. The region is so remote that rumors of "lost" Maori tribes, never encountered by Europeans, persisted until the 1950s. So did reports of surviving moa birds.

Te Anau

Te Anau, an attractive resort based on the tranquil shores of the South Island's largest lake, **Lake Te Anau,** is the best base from which to explore the glorious wilderness of New Zealand's southwest corner. Gateway to the Fiordland National Park, Te Anau is served by both Air New Zealand Link and Ansett NZ Airlines, along with coaches from the West Coast, Christchurch, Dunedin, Queenstown, and Invercargill. A scenic flight over this region, by helicopter, fixed-wing, or amphibious aircraft is breathtaking.

Above the township, high in the Murchison Range, dwell the last of the takahe (*Notornis mantelli*)—flightless birds with brilliant indigo and viridian plumage and a rounded reddish bill. Believed extinct, they were rediscovered in 1948. Thanks to careful conservation, several hundred pairs of takahe thrive in a part of the forest kept strictly out of bounds.

The same day the takahe was found, a new cave was discovered in the area, Te Anau-au ("Cave of Whirling Water"). The only "living" cave in New Zealand, it is still being formed by water rushing in from Lake Orbell. The cave lies across the lake from the town. A quiet night time launch trip makes the perfect introduction. You journey within the cave to an underground waterfall, then to a chamber lit by huge glowworms.

Magnificent Milford Track

The Milford Track, winding through varied and spectacular high country in the South Island, is one of the world's greatest walks. New Zealanders try to experience it at least once in their lifetimes. Safety regulations were introduced several years ago to ensure people walked the track in one direction only. This ensures walkers don't squeeze past each other on narrow stretches, which can be slippery when wet. Each year, some 10,000 people complete the four-day, 55-km (34-mile) bushwalk—yet there are no crowds. If you choose a guided walk, you carry only immediate necessities, staying at comfortable lodges each night.

Walking the track is an undulating and sometimes steep journey past glacier-sided mountains and turquoise lakes, through fields of alpine wildflowers, veils of mist and forests that seem suspended in the era when plants were the only life on earth. Rivers are so transparent you can see big brown trout basking in the shallows, four or five at a time. Each day provides a different type of scenery, from alpine herb fields resembling a botanic garden to rock-strewn mountain passes. There are no four-wheel drives, no mountain bikes, and no roads. The loudest sound is the sighing of the wind and the raucous call of the kea, the world's only alpine parrot.

Manapouri, the country's second deepest lake, (a corruption of *Manawapouri*, "Lake of the Sorrowing Heart"), was saved decades ago when a scheme to raise its level to generate hydro-electricity triggered a storm of public protest. A day trip takes you to the lake and out into Doubtful Sound. You can also visit the West Arm Underground Powerhouse, the country's largest power station. It's probably the world's best concealed—as befits these wondrous surroundings. A tunnel of rough-hewn rock leads down to the plant, 213 m (698 ft) below ground.

Milford Track, believed by many to be the "finest walk in the world," starts at the head of Lake Te Anau. You can rent packs and waterproofs at the Te Anau hotel. Pre-booking is essential.

It's worth stopping at Fiordland National Park Visitor Center, 500 m (1,640 ft) south of Te Anau along Lake Front Drive for information and useful publications.

The Road to Milford

Milford Sound is the best-known and most accessible of the majestic glacier-carved fjords scattered along New Zealand's southwestern coast. Boat trips on the Sound provide close-up views of awe-inspiring scenery. Cruises are often accompanied by playful dolphins.

The road to Milford is one of the world's finest alpine drives. From Te Anau, the road winds down the Eglington and Hollyford valleys, with their superb beech forests, then through the Homer Tunnel to be met by Mitre Peak, towering above the mirror-like surface of Milford Sound. The road winds through patchy tussock, snowgrass, and stretches of gravel, past landscapes of such lonely splendor they evoke a Lost World feel. Pause at the Mirror Lakes to admire the flawless reflections, then follow the Avenue of the Disappearing Mountain—the peak seems to get smaller as you approach, then, suddenly reappears, its snowcapped tip sparkling, its lower slopes daubed with bright mosses and lichens.

On the other side of Knobs Flat, a track leads to Lake Gunn. Lakes Fergus and Lochie are nearby. Pause at Falls Creek, near the Hollyford Valley turnoff, to admire the tumbling cascade. The road then climbs steeply up to Homer Tunnel. The Chasm offers a good view of the meandering Cleddau River. From here, 11 slow, winding, and infinitely rewarding km (6.8 miles) complete the journey to sea level and Milford Sound.

☛ Milford Sound

This may be the rain kingdom of the world. More rain falls on Milford Sound than just about anywhere else in the coun-

Paradise Found: sheer drama awaits at Milford Sound, the best-known fjord of New Zealand's southwestern coast.

try—over 6,000 millimeters (236 inches) a year. It glistens on the trees, lends an ethereal glow to the mosses, sets a thousand waterfalls leaping, and adds to the charm of the surroundings.

No commercial fishing is carried out on Milford Sound, although the salt water contains barracuda, cod, and tuna, and thousands of tiny mussels gleam on the rocks at the water's edge. The fishing boats you see moored in the Sound head for the coast, where the crayfish are huge and succulent.

To leave Milford Sound without taking a launch trip is nearly unthinkable. Clasping your insect repellent firmly in one hand and waving the other vigorously across your face (this is vicious sandfly country), walk or take a shuttle bus to the wharf near Bowen Falls. From your boat you'll see the misty 150-m drop of Stirling Falls, and wonders such as baby seals locking their flippers together in order to float on the surface—or sunbathing on warm grandstand rocks, while dolphins cavort around the boat.

Of all the places you visit in New Zealand, this isolated, ice-carved paradise may well create the strongest and most durable memories.

DUNEDIN AND THE FAR SOUTH

Dunedin, the main center of the Otago Peninsula, is known as the "Edinburgh of the South." The dramatic bush-covered hills and valleys at the head of a long natural harbor first attracted Maori settlers to the site over four centuries ago. European settlement began in 1848, when Scottish migrants established a town and gave it the ancient, Gaelic name for Edinburgh. (Mark Twain wrote of Dunedin in 1895: "The people here are Scots. They stopped on their way home to heaven, thinking they had arrived.") In 1851 gold was discovered about 120 km (74.5 miles) inland, and the little town became the center for the nation's wealth.

Start your tour at the city heart, the Octagon, a square embellished with a statue of the Scots poet Robert Burns. He's portrayed sitting with "his back to the kirk and his face to the pub." In fact, the kirk—St. Paul's Anglican Cathedral—has outlived the pub, which has been demolished.

The dignified Law Courts on Stuart Street provide a dour, sober contrast to the exuberant Railway Station further along. The Otago Early Settlers' Museum nearby displays pioneer and gold-rush mementoes, and the Cargill Monument (High Street), commemorates Captain William Cargill, one of the co-founders of the Free Church of Scotland settlement in Otago.

A soaring spire on the southern side of Moray Place draws the eye to the Neo-Gothic style First Church (1868–73). Knox Church, on George Street, leading from the Octagon, is the work of the same architect, R. A. Lawson.

The Otago Museum (Great King Street) houses an outstanding collection of Maori, Melanesian, and other Pacific Island material, including an ornately carved meeting house.

The imposing Otago University Buildings (Castle Street), constructed of stone and roofed in slate, reflect the importance the city has always placed on education. Olveston House, a gracious Edwardian residence richly decorated with European furniture and objects, was bequeathed to the city by the last surviving member of the cultured and much-traveled Theomin family.

 Some 20 minutes from the city, **Otago Peninsula** is home to a wonderful variety of bird life. Bird-lovers should visit Taiaroa Head at the peninsula's tip, one of the few places in the world where you can see a colony of one of the world's largest birds—the northern royal albatross. Access is strictly controlled. Dunedin's Visitor Center, located in the great stone Municipal Chambers that dominate the Octagon, can supply details.

Otago Peninsula is embellished by two of Dunedin's stately homes: **Glenfalloch,** surrounded by 12 hectares of woodland gardens; and **Larnach's Castle.** The latter, a baronial hall erected in 1871, is enlivened by battlements, a fairy-tale ballroom, and decorative carvings by a British artist who spent 12 years at the task. Larnach's Castle has a tragic history; there's even a ghost.

Invercargill and Environs

A city of wide streets and tree-lined parks, Invercargill was also settled by Scots. New Zealand's most southerly city offers a good art gallery and museum, with audio displays highlighting the fauna and flora of New Zealand's sub-Antarctic islands.

The wild **Catlins Coast,** with its deserted beaches and wind-sculpted outcrops, is home to the rare yellow-eyed penguin and seal colonies. You can walk through a petrified forest and view Cathedral Caves and blowholes.

Bluff, 27 km (16.7 miles) from Invercargill, is known throughout the country for its oysters. From here boats depart for **Stewart Island,** some 30 km (18.6 miles) across Foveaux Strait. Southern Air flights from Invercargill cross Foveaux Strait to land near Oban on Stewart Island. The flight takes 20 minutes, and a bus transports passengers to town. You can also reach Stewart Island on a catamaran ferry from Bluff.

Stewart Island is largely uninhabited, save for Oban, (population 600) at the head of Halfmoon Bay. The little settlement boasts some shops and motels, a camping ground, and a museum. The island possesses just 16 km (10 miles) of paved road and little commerce, a few farmers, a storekeeper or two, and a few fishermen. This, in many ways, is the end of the world. Place names are delightful: Chew Tobacco Bay, Big and Little Hellfire Beaches, Dead Man Beach, and Faith, Hope, and Charity islands. You can explore the northern part of the island—but the south is almost untouched, so don't go far without adequate advice.

WHAT TO DO

SHOPPING

Souvenirs. Quality souvenirs are readily available in New Zealand, and you don't have to resort to kitsch. Superb **Maori carvings** in wood, bone, and greenstone head the list. **Greenstone**, a kind of jade, ranges in hue from pale to dark green. You'll find it carved into simple, tasteful pendants, bracelets, cufflinks, rings, and letter openers and used in the handles of coffee spoons and paring knives. Jewelry and ornaments made from **paua shell** are also popular. An iridescent shell shot through with green and blue, paua is similar to abalone but more colorful. Variations on the traditional **Maori fishhook** look best worn suspended on a flax or leather thong. **Bone** is similarly worked (many New Zealanders wear these around the neck). Rich, golden kauri gum and petrified wood are sometimes mounted in pendants.

Crafts. New Zealand is a craft haven. The country's potters (ceramicists) are recognized as among the world's finest. Other artisans work in stone, wood, glass, and metals. Nelson, Coromandel, Bay of Islands, and Whangarei are major craft centers: in any of these locations you'll be able to watch and learn before buying from local craftspeople. Artisans turn New Zealand timber into articles such as bowls, plates, goblets, trays, bookends, and, for children, attractive chunky toys, puzzles, inlaid rulers, and pencil-boxes. You'll encounter smooth golden kauri, attractively grained reddish rimu, brown rata, and dark hinau. Small items, especially vases, are also made out of ponga (fernwood).

Leather and Skins. New Zealand has a thriving leather industry. Possum and deer skins are fashioned into coats, bags,

Blue skies, charm, and plenty of quality merchandise:
what more could any ardent shopper ask for?

and hats. Chamois is shaped into soft, elegant clothing. And you don't have to feel guilty about the ecology: The deer multiply fast and are culled to protect the forests; they are also farmed.

You won't find better **sheepskins** anywhere. The selection ranges from single pelts to rugs. They are fashioned into carseat covers, coats, boots, and hats and come in natural white, brown, and black, as well as artificial colors. Natural fleece under-blankets are ideal for babies and invalids, as they allow air to circulate. Sheepskin products are stringently tested and you can have confidence if the tag says "machine washable."

Wine and Spirits. A bottle or two of New Zealand wine or a bottle of New Zealand whisky can also make good souvenirs. **Wilsons** is New Zealand's own whisky brand. Pure water, good peat, and inherited Scottish know-how combine to produce a creditable drop.

A jet-boat ride at Wakatipu: the perfect way to get that New Zealand sporting thrill without having to work up a sweat.

Taxes

All goods and services in New Zealand are subject to a 12.5 percent **Goods and Services Tax** (GST), which is included in the displayed price. Visitors cannot claim refunds on this tax, but GST is not charged on either the goods or the freight shipped by a supplier to a visitor's home address.

SPORTS

New Zealand is a physically active country. Everybody seems to play tennis, football, or hockey, skate or ski, jump, jog, hurl a discus, dive, or do gymnastics. The country produces more than its share of Olympic champions—the current Olympic focus is on swimming and equestrian events—and Team New Zealand currently holds yachting's prestigious America's Cup, due to be defended in the seas off Auckland, with challenger trials starting in late 2002 and continuing into 2003.

Kiwis also play tennis, netball, basketball, hockey, and golf on the world stage, and enjoy about every other sport on beaches, in parks, and at clubs throughout the country. But New Zealand's national sport, followed with near-religious fervor, is **rugby**. This has been played passionately in New Zealand for 100 years, and it verges on a national obsession. The national team is the **All Blacks**. To wear the hallowed black uniform, adorned with New Zealand's silver fern motif, is the ambition of sporting schoolboys throughout the land. Becoming an All Black is considered an achievement so mighty that all of life's previous and subsequent accomplishments pale into insignificance. Needless to say, the All Blacks are very good. They are usually at the top of the world league or very close to the top. If you enjoy watching a fast, physical, rough-and-tumble sporting contest played without protection of body-armor, don't miss the opportunity to see a rugby match. The All Blacks play international matches April through October in Auckland, Wellington, Christchurch, and Dunedin.

Many Kiwis are more than just fit, they're tough. It isn't always wise to emulate them. If you're undertaking one of the country's celebrated walks or raft trips, remember that exposure can be dangerous. New Zealanders accustomed to such exertions may get away with facing untamed nature in shorts and boots, but you may need more gear.

Participatory Sports

Golf

Golf is played year-round in New Zealand, which boasts more than 300 registered golf clubs. Private clubs accord guest courtesies to members of clubs overseas; bring along a letter of introduction from your home-club secretary. Every town has public courses, which vary greatly in quality and in chal-

No caddy? No worries! At Taupo's practice range, the object is to aim for the water.

lenges. The initial challenge may be in pronouncing the name of the course.

Rotorua's **Arikikapaka-pa** course sees golfers deftly sidestepping natural blasts of thermal steam and bubbling mud-pools. If your ball disappears into a boiling hazard, don't use your hand to retrieve it. At the **Paraparaumu Beach Golf Club** near Wellington, sea spray and coastal breezes add extra zest to the lie of the course. Tiger Woods played here early in 2002. Many South Island courses are so scenically spectacular that mountain views can distract you from your swing.

New Zealand is an inexpensive country in which to play golf. Green fees range from NZ$10 to an average NZ$30 and NZ$70–$100 at top courses. Greens are generally kept to a high standard year round, though fairways can dry over summer on non-irrigated courses. Most clubs have resident professionals and hire out equipment and caddies. Motorized golf buggies are often available, costing NZ$15–$30. The major competition season runs during the winter/spring months of May to October and courses can be surprisingly quiet during the best weather. The luxury **Formosa Auckland Country Club** boasts the country's longest PGA-rated course, at over 6,600 m. **Millbrook Resort** near Queenstown is another top venue. Both Millbrook and Formosa were designed by Bob Charles, one of New Zealand's premier golfers. Another world-class development is **Gulf Harbour** (that's Gulf, not Golf), near Auckland, designed by Robert Trent-Jones, Jr. It hosted the 1998 World Cup of Golf.

Tennis and Bowls

New Zealanders are practically born with a tennis racket in their hand. The season runs from October to May. Every district has a club, and you'll be given a warm welcome at any of them. Many retired New Zealanders take up bowls, played outdoors on meticulously maintained lawns. Tradition decrees appropriate apparel: white flannels and Panama hat for men, over-the-knee sports dress and hat for women. Younger players are taking an interest in the game, but it's mainly an older persons' pursuit.

Water Sports

There's little you can do in water that isn't available in New Zealand. Always within easy reach of the sea (or a lake or a river), Kiwis are enormously fond of water sports. Swimming, surfing, and sailing count among the most popular water sports—even though the sea seldom gets really warm (it can usually be described as "bracing"). When swimming, take the usual precaution of staying near other people. Heed warnings on dangerous beaches. Drownings are a tragic feature of summertime, but common sense should keep you out of trouble. Take adequate precautions against sunburn—the ultra-violet content of the light can be high.

Sailing

Boating season runs from November to May. Some companies charter fully-equipped yachts, with or without crew. The **Bay of**

Islands, and **Whangaroa** to the north, is a great yachting venue. At the other end of the country, the southern lakes—**Te Anau** and **Whakatipu**—offer exhilarating cooler-climate experiences. The **Hauraki Gulf** (Auckland), **Port Nicholson** (Christchurch), and **Otago Harbour** (Dunedin) are all popular yacht basins.

Fishing

Game fish abound in New Zealand's offshore waters. Lake and stream fishing is just as good. In the sea, you can go after black and striped marlin, broadbill or mako, thresher, hammerhead and blue shark, yellowtail and five other species of tuna during the deep-sea fishing season (mid-January through April). Bases are at Whangaroa, Bay of Islands, Whangarei (Tutukaka), Mercury Bay (Whitianga), Tauranga (Mayor Island), and Whakatane (Whale Island and White Island).

There are no closed-season restrictions for saltwater fishing, and no fishing license is required. Summer (November–April) is best, when the water is warmer and schools of fish run closer to shore. Fishing with light tackle from the shoreline or boats is popular. Guides supply necessary tackle, usually spinning-type outfits smaller than the equipment used for big game fishing. Native New Zealand species include kahawai, snapper, skipjack tuna, yellowtail, terakihi, pink maomao, and blue maomao. Sports shops are usually full of advice.

The **Bay of Islands** is the best-known base for game fishing. The Bay of Islands is the marlin capital of New Zealand and **Whakatane** is the tuna capital. Charters from other ports are available. The best time of year for these spots is January–March, when smaller fish, on which the game fish feed, are borne by warm currents closer to shore. The top fish to go for include the striped marlin, a renowned fighter; New Zealand has the largest in the world. Broadbill is the rarest and most prized of game fish. Night-fishing excursions can prove extraordinarily successful. Mako sharks, ferocious and agile, are reasonably plentiful and can be caught all year. The mako normally puts up an incredible acrobatic display. Saltwater fly-fishing has a following, the main quarry being the kahawai fish.

A limit of four fish per day applies to fish of the sword family, and swordfish can be taken only by rod and line. Modern, high-speed charter launches can accommodate from one to six people; many have flying bridges. The captain provides tackle. If you use your own (excellent tackle is on sale in New Zealand), remember it must comply with International Game Fishing Association rules.

Freshwater fishing is justly renowned. Rainbow and brown trout were released into the country's waters in the 19th century and have proliferated. Novices bring in whoppers every year. Trout are plentiful but catching them is by no means easy. Fly-fishing for brown trout requires different techniques to those used in most other places. Often, the fish must be stalked in clear water. Light tackle and long leaders add a whole new perspective. Trout are generally caught with 1.4 or 1.8 kg (3- or 4-lb) lines.

If it's **salmon** you're after, you'll have to go to the South Island, where quinnat and king salmon lurk, weighing in at 3.6 to 18 kg (8 to 40 lbs). The best salmon haunts are Rakaia, Rangitata, and Waitaki on the east coast; guides and advice are available for each of those areas in Christchurch. There are some fairly good runs of salmon into Dunedin Harbour.

Certain areas are set aside for **fly-fishing.** If not specified, they are open to trolling, thread-lining, and bait-casting. Fly-fishing rods should be reasonably rigid in order to cast into the wind and handle heavy fish. Imported or locally made tackle can be bought or hired. It's best to select flies on site. If possible, bring your own chest or thigh-waders (unless you want to buy a new pair)—they are not always available for rent.

Catch limits vary, but you can count on six to ten rainbow trout per angler per day, and any number of brown trout. Size limits vary too. Generally, anything under 35 cm (about one foot) must be returned. Experienced guides with cars and launches are available in the main angling areas. Helicopters can take you to out-of-the-way fishing spots.

Licenses are required only for trout and salmon fishing. A license purchased in any district allows you to fish anywhere in the country except Taupo, where a separate license is required. In 2002, a day license cost NZ$12, and a week license cost NZ$25 and a seasons license cost $65. To fish Lake Taupo, you must buy a local license which costs $13 per day or $25 a week.

For more information, contact the New Zealand Professional Fishing Guides Association (PO Box 16, Motu, Gisborne, New Zealand; tel: (06) 863-5822, fax: (06) 863-5844). www.flyfishing.net.nz.

River-Rafting

River-rafting in an inflatable rubber boat is a great experience—provided you're fit. You can enjoy a couple of hours of thrills or, if you're an enthusiast, spend several days rafting, camping onshore as you go. The high excitement of negotiating white-water rapids—maneuvering bends and plunging down waterfalls—alternates with passages of placid paddling.

Organized rafting tours are accompanied by guides graded by the New Zealand Professional Rafting Association. They are knowledgeable about their respective regions, and they can also cook and can administer first-aid if necessary. Life jackets and crash helmets are provided.

To participate, you must be able to swim. Depending on the weather, you should wear a wet-suit or woolen clothing (jeans and cotton aren't recommended). Rivers are graded according to difficulty. Some tours combine rafting with other activities—hiking, fishing, even panning for gold. A specialized spin-off is **black-water rafting,** which is similar, but conducted in caves. Not for the faint-hearted!

Hiking

New Zealand has thousands of km of trails (known as "tracks") suitable for hiking (known as "tramping"). You can opt for a guided walk with comfortable accommodation or walk the same route independently. Or you can leave the beaten track and head into the wilderness, staying in a choice of over 1,000 outback country huts.

Kayaking enthusiasts flock to Kawarau Gorge.

The standard of these huts ranges from trim and cozy to somewhat spartan. The cost of staying in track-side huts ranges from NZ$6 to NZ$12 per person per night. The huts on the Milford and Routeburn tracks are plusher and costlier.

Wherever you choose to hike, you'll be rewarded with magnificent landscapes—clear lakes and tumbling waterfalls, grottoes of tree-ferns, unspoiled forests, and native birds. People of all ages can manage the less arduous routes, but don't overestimate your endurance.

The 53-km (33-mile) **Milford Track** on the South Island is the best known walking track, but there's a big choice throughout the country, including the 40-km (25-mile) **Routeburn,** the 27-km (16.7-mile) **Hollyford,** and the 30-km (18.5-mile) **Abel Tasman Coast Track.** Many of the routes traverse superb national parks. Accommodation are more expensive (but of better quality) on the Milford and Routeburn tracks, the country's two most popular.

The Abel Tasman Coastal Track, an easy three- to five-day coastal walk in the Nelson area, is ideal for family groups. The track is open all year and five huts are available. Guided walks run all year round. A boat can drop off or pick up visitors at any beach along the coast.

Heaphy Track is also open all year. This 77-km (48-mile) trek takes four to six days and is suitable for anyone of average physical fitness. It winds through Nelson's Kahurangi National Park, where more than half of all New Zealand's native plant species flourish. The forest finally opens to the wild shore of the West Coast.

Kepler Track, operating from late October to April, is a diverse four-day circuit of Fiordland. The track can be attempted all year round but the alpine section can be closed by snow in winter.

Lake Waikaremoana Track is a 51-km (31.6-mile) three- to four-day trek in remote Te Urewera National Park, the largest tract of native forest in the North Island. Walking is moderately easy, you can swim or fish en route, and the highest point (1,100 m/ 3,666 ft above sea level) offers panoramic lake and Pacific Ocean views.

Milford Track, stretching 54 km (33.5 miles) through a World Heritage Area from the northern end of Lake Te Anau to Milford Sound, runs from the end of October to mid April.

Rakiura Track on Stewart Island, a two- to three-day forest and coastal circuit, is open all year round and suitable for anyone who is moderately fit. The track follows the open coast, ascending rimu and kamahi forest country, then skirts the shores of Paterson Inlet.

Routeburn Track, a challenging 39-km (24-mile) three-day track in Fiordland, is often combined with the adjoining **Greenstone Track** to form a five-day journey called **The Grand Traverse.** Guided walks are available from November to April. In winter, the track becomes hazardous for all but experienced alpine travelers.

Hunting

Game animals can be stalked year-round, without license and generally without limit, although a permit is required to hunt on land managed by the Department of Conservation.

Many game animals—along with smaller animals like the rabbit and the Australian possum—were introduced to New Zealand by early settlers. A 19th-century organization called the Acclimatisation Society set about importing the wildlife that settlers had been familiar with in Britain. Some of these creatures acclimatized so rapidly they became pests. You can bag red deer and fallow deer (common over much of the country), wapiti elk (in mountainous areas of Fiordland), sika deer (one of the most difficult deer species to hunt), rusa deer (restricted to a small area of Urewera National Park), sambar deer (now under protection and requiring a hunting permit, selected by ballot), whitetail (on Stewart Island), Himalayan thar (found high in the mountains of central South Island), Austrian chamois (in the South island mountains), South Pacific goat (released by early whalers and sealers for food, should they become shipwrecked), and wild sheep. You can also hunt feral pigs—lean, dark, aggressive hogs known as Captain Cook razorbacks, or "Captain Cookers," after the navigator who introduced their ancestors. Smaller game animals include rabbit, hare, opossum, and wallaby.

When hunting, it's best to use a guide. They work either in the wild or on their own protected lands. The charges vary, but NZ$450 per day is a reasonable estimate; this usually includes food, equipment, and accommodation, plus a trophy fee when an animal is shot. To hunt by yourself in the wilderness, you'll need a permit to carry a firearm in State Forests (usually available free from the Department of Conservation). Rifles of .270 caliber or larger are recommended. A permit is required to bring any firearm into New Zealand; you can obtain one upon arrival from the police after making a declaration to Customs officers and paying a fee. Concealable firearms, such as revolvers and automatic pistols, are prohibited.

The seasons for game birds, waterfowl, pheasant, and quail are limited, and licenses are required.

Skiing and Snow-Boarding

Both the North and South Islands offer skiers large areas of alpine terrain, plenty of powder snow, and a season (July–October) that conveniently coincides with the Northern Hemisphere's summer. The country operates 12 commercial ski areas, each of which offers qualified ski schools, rental equipment, child care, and quality dining facilities. Lift passes range from about NZ$35 to NZ$60; equipment rental is about NZ$28 a day for skis, boots and poles, and about NZ$40 for snowboards. Lessons start at about NZ$30 for a half-day group class.

North Island skiing centers include **Mt. Ruapehu,** in Tongariro National Park, and **Turoa,** site of the highest vertical ski lift in Australasia (720 m/ 2,360 ft). On the South Island, **Mt. Hutt** has an exceptionally long season, while **Tekapo** is sunny, with good powder snow. **Wanaka** offers exceptional scenery; **Tasman Glacier** offers helicopter lifts to virgin snow for experienced skiers. **Coronet Peak,** close to Queenstown, ranks among the world's best ski fields. Experienced skiers

Admire the vistas from a Queenstown gondola—or jump right into them with a bungee cord tied around your ankle.

can try glacier skiing or the new "snow-cat skiing," which makes use of snow groomers to access untracked slopes over the back of the **Remarkables Range** in Queenstown.

South Island ski slopes became more accessible in 1998 with the completion of a new NZ$72-million international terminal at Christchurch Airport, specially designed to handle skiers and snow-boarders and their equipment on the flights from Christchurch to Queenstown. The domestic transfer terminal has been relocated inside the international arrivals hall, allowing travelers to check in skis, snowboards, and luggage immediately instead of having to lug gear through the terminal. In the baggage-claim hall, a conveyor and storage rack for handling ski equipment ensures fast and efficient delivery to passengers.

Spectator Sports

Rugby and Soccer

Rugby (the most popular form of football) and soccer matches draw crowds from June through October. Rugby League, the code played in Australia, has a growing following. You'll need to make reservations for the major matches. (Cricket is played in the summer months.)

Horse-Racing

New Zealanders are dedicated horse-racing fans. The country's world-famous thoroughbreds include the formidable galloper Phar Lap, foaled in the South Island town of Timaru. In the Depression years, Phar Lap defeated all challengers in New Zealand, Australia, and America. The racehorse gained such prestige that Australian Prime Minister Joseph Lyons called its death in 1932 "a great tragedy."

In addition to "gallops," trotting events and greyhound races often take place at night under floodlighting. Off-course bets can be placed at authorized TAB (Totalisator Agency Board) offices in all centers, www.tab.co.nz or by telephone.

Wilder Options

Some of New Zealand's newer adventure activities are pretty rugged, if not dangerous. The country that invented bungee-jumping and jetboating has now produced Zorb and Argo. These are not rock musicians or Hells Angels, but ways of having fun (theoretically, anyway).

The **Zorb** is a giant plastic ball. Riders, called Zorbonauts, dive into the middle of the Zorb and roll downhill. Centrifugal force plasters the Zorbonaut to the walls of his or her Zorb. The sport has been around for some time, but re-

Maori concerts include a little music, a little hand-to-hand combat, and a big insight into the intricacies of the culture.

finements in the terrain are always being made.

The **Argo** is an eight-wheel-drive, amphibious, all-weather, all-terrain vehicle—highly maneuverable and versatile, hurtling through mud, through forests, across rivers, and up near-vertical escarpments.

If you want to bungee-jump, why not try the latest variant and do so from Auckland's Sky Tower? There is a controlled base operating 192m (630 ft) up the Southern Hemisphere's tallest structure (www.skyjump.co.nz).

ENTERTAINMENT

Entertainment in New Zealand cities includes theater, discos, late-night cafés, and live-music venues. Smaller towns tend to be quiet after dark. Hotels and restaurants in larger cities feature good bands and name entertainers. In

Calendar of Events

Here is a list of the major annual festivals and national events in New Zealand. Exact dates should be confirmed through local tourist offices.

January: Anniversary Regatta, Auckland (final weekend of the month). Summer City Program, Wellington (two months of entertainment lasting to end of February). Taste Nelson, Nelson, annual food and wine festival (first Saturday). Garden City Festival, Christchurch (first Saturday).

February: Air New Zealand Wine and Food Festival, Marlborough (second weekend). Art Deco Festival, Napier (third weekend). International Festival of the Arts, Wellington (held on even-numbered years).

March: Golden Shears Sheep Shearing Competition, Masterton (you must have shorn more than 410 sheep in a day to compete.). Ngaruwahia Regatta for Maori Canoes, Hamilton. ECNZ Waitaki River Salmon Fishing Contest, Waimate. Wildfoods Festival, Hokitika. Pasifika, Auckland, celebration of Polynesian arts and culture.

April: Highland Games, Hastings. Royal New Zealand Easter Show, Auckland. Gumboot Day, Taihape, gumboot-throwing competition (Easter Tuesday).

May: Rotorua Marathon, Rotorua, NZ's oldest and most popular.

June: New Zealand Agricultural Field Days, Hamilton.

August: Bay of Islands Jazz and Blues Festival.

September: New Zealand Trout Festival, nationwide. Hastings Blossom Festival, Hastings, celebrating the arrival of spring. Wearable Art Awards, Nelson, oddball fashion/art event in middle of Nelson Arts Festival week.

October: Rhododendron Festival, Dunedin.

November: Canterbury Show Week, Canterbury.

December: Festival of Lights, New Plymouth, lighting display and musical event in beautiful Pukekura Park

Wellington, cafés on Cuba Street sometimes offer live music well into the early hours. Wellington is the best place for live theater.

If you enjoy gambling, try one of the casinos in Christchurch or in Auckland, where the Sky City casino complex also includes five restaurants, three bars, and a theater.

Cinema flourishes: New Zealand has a thriving film industry. In 2001, New Zealand filmmaker Peter Jackson stunned the world with the first film of his 'Lord of the Rings' trilogy. He made history by being the first person to direct three major feature films simultaneously. The second and third films will be released in 2002 and 2003 respectively. Other internationally recognised NZ directors include Jane Campion, Vincent Ward, Lee Tamahori and Roger Donaldson.

Don't miss the **Maori concerts** in Rotorua. The performers enjoy them as much as the audience. You'll see young girls performing graceful poi dances (the poi is a fiber ball twirled on a length of twine), stick games, and action dances. The men demonstrate hand games devised to train warriors for alertness in battle, and will do their best to scare the wits out of you with a haka.

You're also likely to hear some so-called **Maori songs**. Delightful as they sound, most of this music has been Europeanized quite a bit. In early times the musical range was smaller and the main instrument was a type of flute. The concerts are well commentated in several languages; they are very relaxed, and sooner or later everybody joins in.

Away from large towns, look out for the **agricultural shows**, which often feature show-jumping, home made produce stalls plus typical New Zealand competitions like ax-chopping, sheep-shearing, and sheep-dog trials, which involve a fascinating display of telepathy between master and dog.

EATING OUT

What to Eat

Traditional British eating habits held sway until a few years ago, when the pendulum swung the other way, triggering widespread experimentation. New Zealand has the benefit of superb natural ingredients—a wide variety of freshwater and saltwater fish, game, and farmed meat of all types, as well as abundant fresh fruit and vegetables. Treating this bounty with due respect can produce superlative results, and in cities and larger towns, quality cafés and restaurants now offer cuisine from all continents. Subtle and distinctive tastes are evolving into a recognizable national style that incorporates influences from California and Asia as well as hints of French nouvelle cuisine.

New Zealanders have always enjoyed meat. Lamb, beef, and chicken are all excellent, and farmed venison (marketed as "cervena") makes regular appearances at restaurant tables.

The Hangi

Every visitor to New Zealand should try to sample a Maori feast: a scrumptious spread of meats and seafood prepared in an open-air oven known as a hangi. (The word hangi also applies to any social gathering where hangi-cooked food is eaten.) A big pit is dug in the ground and heated stones are placed at the bottom. The food, enclosed in flax bags, is lowered in, covered with leaves, wet cloths, and a layer of earth, and allowed to steam. Although the accent is on Maori favorites such as smoked eel, fish, mussels, and a small shellfish known as the pipi, European tastes are admitted, too: you'll also encounter hangi feasts that feature tender suckling pig, chicken, lamb, and venison.

Local ingredients such as fresh seafood and vegetables make for a refreshing picnic by the shore.

Yugoslav immigrants planted some of the country's first vineyards, many of which now successfully produce high-quality wines, including Chardonnays, Pinot Noirs, Sauvignon Blancs, and other varieties. Some restaurants possess full liquor licenses, others are unlicensed. Some carry a BYO sign ("Bring Your Own")—the waiters are happy to serve the wine you bring into the restaurant and will even keep your wine on ice if it requires chilling.

Most towns of any size boast a wide variety of eating-places serivng cuisine from around the world—French, Italian, Chinese, Indian, and Indonesian—but small towns may be limited to take-away food and basic cafés. International fast-food chains are well represented, as are vegetarian and health-food establishments. Living as they do in the lap of gastronomic plenty, many New Zealanders try to be diet-conscious.

Diet aside, **take-away stalls** specializing in fresh **fish and chips, deep-fried oysters and mussels,** or **paua fritters** can provide you with a regal repast. You'll be surprised how delicious Kiwi fish and chips can taste when eaten al fresco out of newspaper by the seashore—particularly when accompanied by a cold beer or a crisp dry white wine.

Pubs serve simple, filling meals (offering good value at lunch-time); coffee shops and wine bars offer sandwiches and simple hot dishes. American-style hamburgers and milkshakes are popular—but beware of so-called "hot dogs," which here consist of a sausage covered in batter, deep-fried, skewered on a stick, and, customarily, doused in ketchup.

Soups and Starters

In New Zealand, the term "entrée" on a restaurant menu means a starter. The main course is usually called just that: "main." The superb selection of fish and shellfish available in New Zealand includes varieties found nowhere else, such as the **toheroa,** a type of clam. These shellfish are dug with wooden spades from certain beaches during a restricted winter season. The toheroa can be baked in its shell, minced, coated in pastry and fried, or, most often, made into a rich, strong soup. Look, too, for its close cousin, the smaller, sweeter **tuatua.**

Seafood pâtés, including crayfish and smoked eel, can be excellent. Perhaps sample a starter made from **terakihi,** a firm-fleshed sea fish marinated in lemon juice and served Polynesian-style in coconut milk.

Seafood

New Zealand waters teem with fish and shellfish. Fishermen bring in excellent **scallops, crayfish**, and **oysters** by the boatload, as well as **flounder, sole,** and delicately flavored **John Dory.** Restaurant menus feature **snapper,** the most plentiful variety, and **grouper** (hapuka), a popular deep-water species. Kingfish is prized but not widely available. Sample densely textured **ling,** baked or steamed. You'll also come across **piper** (best fried), **bonito** (served in steaks), **squid,** and smoke-cured **marlin.**

Freshwater rivers produce delicate little **whitebait,** which are usually delectably pan-fried in butter. You may eat **sockeye** and **quinnat salmon** in restaurants, but not brown or rainbow trout, since they are classified as game fish. An eccentric law bans the purchase or sale of trout. Some restaurants will cook it for you if you catch your own.

Meat and Game

The traditional Kiwi favorite, **lamb,** still comes out tops, tender and fragrantly seasoned. New Zealanders prefer it roasted and served with mint sauce or mint jelly, British style. This dish often serves as Christmas dinner. Try crown of lamb with a tangy tamarillo sauce. Prepared well, this garnet-colored subtropical fruit proves the perfect complement. **Suckling pig** and **wild boar** are excellent. **Quail** and **pheasant** are sometimes served with mountain berries.

Fruits and Vegetables

While pineapple, papaya (pawpaw), mangoes, coconuts, avocados, and bananas are widely used, they are all imported. **Passion fruit, kiwifruit, oranges,** and **tangelos** (a delicious cross between a mandarin and a grapefruit) are all grown locally. You may also encounter **feijoas,** a small green semi-tropical fruit. Apples, pears, peaches, cherries, apricots, and nectarines thrive in various regions. In season, you can enjoy luscious strawberries, raspberries, cherries, and blackberries.

New Zealand's corner cafés offer a square meal—and a chance to watch the local goings-on as well.

All the familiar vegetables are grown in New Zealand—from leeks, lettuces, and cauliflower to capsicums (green peppers). Thanks to the benign climate, vegetables tend to grow larger and have a stronger flavor than in Europe. Perhaps experiment with the native **kumara** (sweet potato) and **kumi-kumi** (a type of pumpkin). The sublime taste of fresh New Zealand **asparagus** is a wonder crying out to be sampled.

Cheese and Butter

New Zealand's celebrated dairy products include yogurt and excellent cheeses. Among the latter, there's a choice of cheddar (mild or tangy), Camembert, Brie, blue-vein, Greek-style feta (packed in brine), and port-wine and smoked cheese, as well as cheeses and spreads flavored with herbs, chives, or sesame. Try New Zealand cheese with locally produced crispbreads, crackers, and breads, including long French loaves and whole-grain products. Those contented-looking cows you see contribute to the quality of the butter: it owes its yellow color to the rich carotene content of the grass, not to any additives.

Desserts

Sample the delicious rich **ice cream,** especially the subtropical fruit flavors. Cakes and pastries layered with fresh whipped cream culminate in the long-established national favorite, **Pavlova.** This mammoth meringue, slightly sticky on the inside and crisp on the outside, topped with cream and decorated with fruit. **Cheesecakes** are also popular, and British visitors will warm to home treats like treacle pudding and hot apple pie well studded with cloves.

Drinks

Pubs in New Zealand are often called "hotels" (whether or not they offer accommodation) and liquor stores are known as "bottle shops." Some pubs are still divided, along British lines, into a rougher public bar (where you can dress more or less as you please, and which tend to be male hang-outs) and a more genteel lounge bar that enforces a dress code.

Draft beer, often on the weak side and fairly flat, is served in one-liter jugs or smaller glasses. Bottled brews are generally better: Top brands include **Steinlager** and boutique varieties like **Black Mac** (brewed in Nelson).

New Zealand **white wines** are excellent and reds are rapidly improving. Solid, beefy Australian reds feature on many wine lists, along with imported brands from France, Italy, the US, and other countries.

Tea is widely consumed, but **coffee** is more popular, and stylish coffee bars have sprung up in most cities and in larger towns.

HANDY TRAVEL TIPS

An A–Z Summary of Practical Information

A

ACCOMMODATION (see also CAMPING, YOUTH HOSTELS, and the list of RECOMMENDED HOTELS)

New Zealand has a full range of accommodation, from campsites and budget hotels to luxury resorts, but it's a good idea to book in advance if you plan to stay in major tourist areas in peak season, when New Zealanders take holidays en masse: the summer break from Christmas to the end of January, and Easter.

Top-class international-standard hotels cost from NZ$200 to NZ$1000 a night, although cheaper deals are usually available. Chain hotels include well-known names like Hyatt, Copthorne, Sheraton, Novotel, and Ibis. Exclusive retreats and sporting lodges, a category in which New Zealand excels, can cost from NZ$400 to NZ$1100 a night, including meals. They are generally built amid magnificent scenery in tranquil mountain, lakeside, forest, or seaside locations. The service is exceptional and the management can arrange professional guides for most activities. Delightful and distinctive older-style guesthouses can be enjoyed at very reasonable rates.

Medium-class hotels and motor inns costs between NZ$80 and NZ$250 per night for a double. You can expect a house bar, en-suite bathrooms, and probably a restaurant.

Motels and motor inns are ideal if you're on a driving holiday. They offer single rooms and family suites. Most have restaurants with licenses to serve alcohol. They generally cost from NZ$50 to NZ$150 a night, for a double room, with price depending on size and location. Better motels usually have one or two bedrooms, living room, bathroom, and fully-equipped kitchen. Larger ones may offer a swimming pool. Most also have laundry facilities, refrigerators, cookers, crockery, cutlery, and essentials like instant coffee, tea, milk, and sugar. In units where cooking facilities are not provided, breakfast is included.

Farm holidays provide a glimpse of the real New Zealand. Hosts provide three meals a day and guests can explore, ride, fish, swim, or help out on the farm. They run about NZ$120 to NZ$400 a night for a double. You'll share home-cooked meals with your hosts, who can tell you about local outdoor activities.

New Zealand

AIRPORTS

Auckland (AKL) International. 22 km (13.5 miles) south of the city center. Transport to city by taxi or bus (45 minutes).

   Christchurch (CHC) International. 10 km (6.2 miles) northwest of the city center. Transport to city by taxi or bus (25 minutes).

   Wellington (WLG) International. 8 km (5 miles) southeast of the city center. Transport to city by taxi or bus (15 minutes).

   Long-haul international flights generally land in Auckland. Trans-Tasman flights from Australia also serve Wellington, Auckland, and Christchurch, with additional direct air links between Australia and smaller centers such as Queenstown, Hamilton, Dunedin and Palmerston North. All the major airports have baggage trolleys, hotel reservation desks, car-rental offices, banks, information centers, and souvenir and duty-free shops. A departure tax of NZ$20 currently applies if leaving from Dunedin; NZ$22 from Auckland; NZ$25 from Christchurch, Wellington, Hamilton and Palmerston North. This charge is assessed to everyone over the age of 12 leaving the country and must be paid in New Zealand currency. This is not included in the ticket price; it must be paid at the airport, so make sure you keep some cash handy to cover it. (See also CUSTOMS AND ENTRY REQUIREMENTS.)

B

BICYCLE RENTAL

New Zealand's quiet roads and stunning scenery make it ideal for cycle touring—provided you can cope with a few hills. Bikes can be rented for NZ$15 to NZ$35 a day; some specialist cycle shops can arrange more economical rentals from about NZ$200 a month for a standard touring bike in good condition. Ten-speed bikes and tandems can be hired for sightseeing in most cities. Safety helmets are compulsory, so bring your own if you don't want to buy one in New Zealand or go through the hassle of trying to rent one that fits. Outlets in resorts such as Queenstown and Taupo also have mountain bikes for rent. Guided cycle tours ranging from six to 18 days are available; on these trips your luggage is transported by van to each lodging along the way. Backpacker transport operators such as Kiwi Experience (Tel: 09/366-9860) can arrange bike rentals and issue vouchers that allow you to transport your bike on their buses when you're not riding. The South Island is flatter than the North Island—apart from the Southern Alps. Most of the eastern South Island is a fairly flat plain and the main city, Christchurch, is a cyclist's paradise.

BUDGETING for YOUR TRIP

New Zealand is not a particularly expensive destination. A hotel breakfast costs about NZ$10 to NZ$25, while a three-course dinner (excluding wine) ranges from NZ$20 to NZ$50. Tasty snacks such as open-face sandwiches are sold in cafés for NZ$5 to NZ$10. A hamburger costs between NZ$3.50 and NZ$5 and a café lunch costs about NZ$10. In Auckland, expect to pay about NZ$3 for a cappuccino.

To send a postcard anywhere out of the country by air mail costs NZ$1.50. A 39-shot roll of Kodak film costs about NZ$10.00. Rental cars range from about NZ$40 to NZ$120 a day, depending on season and the size of the vehicle. Local car-rental firms may charge substantially less than international companies: their cars range from low-quality to luxury limos. Petrol is about NZ$1.05 a liter and diesel is about NZ$0.65 a liter. InterCity, the largest nationwide coach operator, charges around NZ$50 for an Auckland–Bay of Islands trip. Motor camps cost about NZ$15, campsites NZ$6 to $10 per person.

C

CAMPING

Since much of New Zealand's appeal lies out-of-doors, camping is a wonderful way to see the country. Many people rent a caravan (trailer), or, more commonly, a motor home (camper van). Luxury vehicles come equipped with heating and toilet facilities, refrigerators, cookers, and kitchen utensils.

Motor camps near main resorts are well-maintained and come with electricity and toilet and laundry facilities. Campers must provide their own tents and equipment, which is available for rent throughout the country. Some camps offer cabins ranging from the purely basic to the equivalent of a modest apartment. For these you provide your own blankets, linen, and cutlery. Prices vary according to standards and season. Advance reservations are necessary during the peak season (Dec–April) and it's a good idea to book as far in advance as possible.

Camping sites have fewer facilities than motor camps and are located in remoter areas. Ask for the Automobile Association's Motor Camp and Cabin Booklet and the official directory issued by the Camp and Cabin Association of New Zealand. The AA also provides a list of caravan rental companies.

The Department of Conservation (DOC) administers over 260 idyllically located campsites in picturesque spots like national parks. DOC campsites come in three categories: **Serviced** (flush toilets, faucet water, kitchen, laundry, hot showers, garbage collection, picnic tables, and usually some powered sites); **Standard** (toilets, water supply, and vehicle access (sometimes only by boat) maybe barbecues or fireplaces, picnic tables, and garbage collection); and **Informal** (limited facilities—in some cases only running water).

The adult rate per night for a serviced DOC campsite is NZ$6.50 to NZ$8; for a standard campsite NZ$2 to NZ$10. Camping is free in informal camping areas and for children under five. You can book ahead for all serviced campsites by contacting the DOC office or visitor center near the campsite. Standard campsites tend to operate on a first-come first-served basis. Further details on the DOC website—www. doc.govt.nz.

CAR RENTAL

Reliable international and local firms offer a range of vehicles. You'll need an approved national or international driving license. The minimum age is 21, and drivers under 25 sometimes have to pay more for insurance. Major international firms like Avis, Hertz, and Budget have offices in New Zealand, but local firms can often offer cheaper deals. Rental cars range from NZ$40 to $120 per day, with rates fluctuating seasonally and varying according to the length of rental. Camper vans cost from NZ$90 or less in low season to NZ$225 for a six-berth in high season.

Take care: even if you take out collision damage waiver, you can still end up paying for the first NZ$500 or NZ$1000 of any damage to your rental vehicle—whether you are responsible or not for the accident. Some firms let you take out extra insurance to reduce your exposure to this insidious charge.

Chauffeur-driven vehicles are available for short or long trips. Taxi companies also provide the services of experienced driver-guides. Rates include basic mileage plus the driver's living expenses and vary according to the number of passengers. If you rent a mobile home or camper van between May and December, you may benefit from a considerable off-season discount. (See also DRIVING.)

CHILDREN

Apart from particularly strenuous river-rafting trips and hikes, children can participate in most adult activities. Visiting children will find plenty others of their own age anxious to have them join in spontaneous games of cricket, rounders, softball, or football. Even the smallest community has a children's playground. Hotels and motels can provide games for wet-weather amusement. Public bars are prohibited to young people under the age of 18.

Most children find New Zealand a wonderful adventure, with trees to be climbed, creeks to be explored, and animals to be fed and petted—all in a very child-oriented society. But take care that children don't wander off into the bush or swim unattended—even unsupervised paddling can be dangerous on some unprotected ocean beaches. Make sure that children wear life-jackets when boating, and that they stay on the paths in thermal areas. Also note that some appealing-looking native berries are poisonous.

CLIMATE and CLOTHING

New Zealand's climate ranges from subtropical in the northern North Island to temperate/cool in the South Island. Places like Invercargill on the southern coast of the South Island can be bitterly cold in winter, when southerly winds blow up from Antarctica. When planning your trip, remember the seasons are the reverse of those in the Northern Hemisphere: summer runs from December through February; fall from March through May; winter from June through August; and spring from September through November. Although some greetings cards and decorations still pay tribute to Yuletide snow and holly, Christmas comes in summer and you're likely to spend it at the beach, where the "pohutukawa," New Zealand's own Christmas tree, will be in full scarlet flower along the cliffs. Labor Day (fourth Monday in October) heralds the warmer weather. Main school holidays run from mid-December to early February, so make reservations well in advance for this peak period.

In summer (Nov–Feb) conventional lightweight clothing is comfortable, and shorts and tee-shirts are common. Some pubs and hotel bars frown on jeans, thong sandals, and bare feet, and some request that men wear ties.

In mountain and bush areas, prepare for changes in the weather and take appropriate footwear. New Zealanders at leisure often go barefoot, but they're used to it. Walking on sharp shells, prickly lawns, and hot pavements isn't easy for novices. A raincoat and umbrella come in handy. In Wellington, umbrellas may be blown inside out, so stick to coats!

The following chart shows the average daily maximum temperature for each month in Auckland and Christchurch:

		J	F	M	A	M	J	J	A	S	O	N	D
Auckland	°F	74	75	74	68	63	59	58	59	63	64	68	71
	°C	23	24	23	20	17	15	14	15	17	18	20	22
Christchurch	°F	71	71	67	63	57	52	52	54	59	63	67	69
	°C	22	22	19	17	14	11	11	12	15	17	19	21

COMPLAINTS

Your first recourse should be the proprietor of the establishment in question, or your hotel manager, travel agency representative, or tour operator, as appropriate. While there is no public tourism watchdog, New Zealand has both a Minister of Tourism and a Minister of Consumer Affairs. In the unusual event of your being unable to obtain satisfaction, write to PO Box 1473, Wellington, New Zealand; Tel: (04) 474 2750.

CRIME and SAFETY

If you take reasonable precautions, there is no reason to expect trouble. Lock your car and don't leave tempting articles visible inside. Make sure camper vans are well secured. Keep valuables in the hotel safe and don't leave possessions on the beach while you swim. Any theft should be reported immediately to hotel authorities, who will then contact the police. Drug offenses, particularly if they relate to harder drugs, are treated very seriously. Marijuana is widely available but remains illegal.

While New Zealand is a safe country, it is unwise for a lone woman to walk at night in some big city areas, such as the "K" Road nightlife area in Auckland. New Zealand has some fearsome-looking motorcycle gangs on the roads, but they are unlikely to hassle tourists. When they fight, it's usually with each other.

CUSTOMS and ENTRY REQUIREMENTS

Passports are required for all visitors. They must be valid for at least three months beyond the date you intend leaving the country. You must obtain a visitor's visa before you travel to New Zealand, unless you are an Australian citizen traveling on an Australian passport, an Australian resident with a current Australian resident return visa, or a citizen of a growing number of countries that now have visa-waiver agreements with New Zealand.

In 2002, these countries included: (for visits of up to 30 days) citizens of France living in Tahiti or New Caledonia; (for visits up to three months) citizens of Andorra, Argentina, Austria, Bahrain, Belgium, Brazil, Brunei, Canada, Chile, Denmark, Finland, France, Germany, Greece, Hong Kong, Hungary, Iceland, Ireland, Israel, Italy, Japan, Kiribati, Kuwait, Liechtenstein, Luxembourg, Malaysia, Malta, Mexico, Monaco, Nauru, Netherlands, Norway, Oman, Portugal, Qatar, San Marino, Saudi Arabia, Singapore, Slovenia, South Africa, South Korea, Spain, Sweden, Switzerland, Tuvalu, United Arab Emirates (UAE), Uruguay, the US, Vatican City and Zimbabwe; (for visits of up to six months) British citizens and other British passport holders who have evidence of the right to live permanently in the United Kingdom.

Every person arriving in New Zealand must complete an arrival card handed out on the aircraft. No vaccination certificates are required. Visitors may be granted entry to New Zealand for up to three months (residents of the UK, six months), a period that may be extended for up to a year for genuine tourists. To gain entry, visitors must hold fully-paid onward or return tickets to a country they have permission to enter and sufficient funds to maintain themselves during their stay in New Zealand (generally considered to be at least NZ$1000 per person per month). Goods up to a total combined value of NZ$700 are free of duty and tax, but goods in excess of this may attract both. If you are over 17 you may also take the following into New Zealand free of duty and tax: 200 cigarettes or 250 grams of tobacco or 50 cigars (or a mixture of all three not weighing more than 250 grams); 4.5 liters of wine (equivalent to six standard 750-ml wine bottles) or 4.5 liters of beer and one 1125-ml bottle of spirits or liqueur.

Animal products, fruit, plant material, or foodstuffs that could contain plant or animal pests and diseases are banned. Heavy fines may be imposed on people caught carrying these. If you have anything that would fit this description, particularly fruit, place it in the bins provided on the approach to the immigration area. Concealable firearms (such as revolvers and automatic pistols) are prohibited. Other types of firearms and ammunition need a license, issued by police officers on arrival. The import of narcotics is prohibited. There is no restriction on the import or export of foreign or local currency. Visitors to New Zealand may purchase duty-free goods, which are not subject to local taxes, from airport duty-free shops upon arrival and departure. Duty-free stores in downtown Auckland, Wellington, and Christchurch will deliver purchases to aircraft departure lounges.

D

DRIVING

Road conditions: Roads are generally good, and light traffic in remoter parts of the country makes driving a pleasure, although roads can be tortuous. Auckland has peak-hour traffic jams.

Rules and Regulations: Provided you hold a valid overseas driver license or an international driving permit, you can drive in New Zealand for up to one year before you are required to apply for a New Zealand license. You must be able to prove you hold a valid overseas license and drive only those types of vehicles for which you were licensed in your country of origin. Carry your license or permit with you whenever you are driving. Traffic keeps to the left. Seat belts are compulsory for all passengers. Helmets are compulsory for motorcyclists and sidecar passengers. Maximum speed limits are 50 km/h (31 mph) in built-up areas unless otherwise indicated, 100 km/h (62 mph) on open roads. Road hazards include possums, quail, flocks of sheep, and herds of cows, so go carefully. If you encounter animals, take your time and edge through them, or get someone to walk ahead to clear a path for the vehicle. Where there are no sidewalks, walk facing the oncoming traffic.

Two facts are worth remembering. First, the driving age in New Zealand is 15, so you may encounter juveniles in control of vehicles. Second, New Zealand has a bizarre and unique road rule that bewilders the uninitiated and has caused more than one visitor to have an accident: You must yield to every vehicle approaching or crossing from your right. This means that even when you are making a simple left-hand turn, a car facing you coming from the opposite direction has the right of way. If you are renting a car, ask the rental agency to explain this peculiar rule fully before you start out—knowledge of it may help save your vehicle or even your life.

Fuel Costs: Prices run at about NZ$1.05 a liter for unleaded, five or six cents more per liter for super-unleaded, and NZ$0.65 for diesel. Fuel is generally cheaper in cities; it's more expensive in country areas.

If You Need Help: The New Zealand Automobile Association offers free services and privileges to members of accredited overseas motoring organizations. It also handles vehicle insurance. Through the Association you can make reservations for accommodation and the inter-island ferry. Check out their website, www.nzaa.co.nz.

Contact one of the following offices:

Auckland: 99 Albert Street; Tel: (09) 377-4660.
Wellington: 342–352 Lambton Quay; Tel: (04) 470-9999.
Christchurch: 210 Hereford St; Tel: (03) 379-1280.

E

ELECTRICITY

230V/50Hz AC is standard. Most hotels have sockets for 110V AC electric razors. The country uses the Australasian/Pacific model plug (three flat pins laid out in a birds-foot pattern).

EMBASSIES

Here is a listing of the principal diplomatic and consular representatives in Wellington:

New Zealand

Australia: *High Commission:* 72–78 Hobson Street, Thorndon (Private Bag); Tel: (04) 473-6411; www.australia.org.nz

Canada: *High Commission:* 61 Molesworth Street (PO Box 12049); Tel: (04) 473-9577; www.wellington.gc.ca

UK: *High Commission:* 44 Hill Street, Thorndon (PO Box 1812); Tel: (04) 924 2888; www.britain.org.nz

US: *Embassy:* 29 Fitzherbert Terrace, Thorndon (PO Box 1190); Tel: (04) 472-2068; www.us.embassy.state.gov/wellington

EMERGENCIES

Dial **111** for police, fire, or ambulance. Emergency numbers for doctors, dentists, hospitals, and local authorities are given in the front of local telephone directories and posted in telephone boxes. Police control call-outs for search-and-rescue services in the bush.

Fire Hazards: Fire poses a constant threat to New Zealand's natural beauty. In summer, scrub and grass are tinder-dry and the slightest spark can start a blaze. Don't throw matches or cigarettes from car windows, and don't light fires in restricted areas. Beach barbecues are tolerated as long as you're a safe distance from trees, but be sure to shelter the fire well from sea breezes a chance cinder can set a whole bush-bound coast alight. Always extinguish a fire carefully by dowsing it with water or covering it with earth. Glass can concentrate the sun's rays and start fires; store empty bottles in the shade and take them with you when you leave.

G

GAY and LESBIAN TRAVELERS

New Zealand is a gay-tolerant country generally, although prejudice persists, particularly in smaller towns. The country has a history of enlightened laws relating to human rights. Homosexuality ceased being categorized as a criminal offense in 1986. The age of consent was set at 16 (the same as for heterosexuals). There are no restrictions on people with HIV or AIDS entering New Zealand.

There are plenty of facilities and activities in New Zealand catering for the gay, lesbian and bisexual traveler, including Gay Ski Week in Queenstown and the Great Party weekend in Wellingon. For further information, contact Gay Tourism New Zealand (04-917-9176 or email: info@gaytourismnewzealand.com) or check out the Gay Travel New Zealand website on www.gaytravel.net.nz.

GETTING to NEW ZEALAND

International Flights. Fares vary widely, so ask an informed travel agent well before departure.

From Australia: Frequent direct flights operated by Air New Zealand and Qantas link Sydney and Auckland each day. Recent developments have seen flight frequency increase, with more services flown by B737 aircraft. These days, Australian airlines view New Zealand as virtually a domestic destination. The same view applies vice versa—though obviously you need appropriate documents to travel between the two countries. Qantas and Air New Zealand offer direct flights to Auckland from major Australian cities, as well as direct flights to Christchurch and Wellington from Brisbane, Melbourne, and Sydney. Freedom Air, an Air New Zealand subsidiary, also links centers on each side of the Tasman Sea.

From Japan: Scheduled flights leave Tokyo for Auckland and Christchurch direct several times a week. One-stop connections are available through Bangkok, Singapore, Bali, and Hong Kong.

From North America: Auckland is linked with Los Angeles by direct, non-stop flights, taking slightly less than 16 hours, on average. Several connections a day run from Auckland to Wellington or Christchurch. New Zealand can also be reached with one or two stops in the Pacific. It can be reached from New York in just two stops and from San Francisco in one stop.

From the British Isles: Regular weekly flights operate from London to New Zealand with one, two, or three stops en route. More than 12 airlines offer these, including Air New Zealand, Qantas, and various Asian carriers. Since the flight lasts at least 24 hours, the cheapest ticket may not be the best deal—it may involve more than one airline and two or more stops, typically requiring you to change aircraft (and possibly airlines) in either Singapore, Hong Kong, Sydney, or Los Angeles.

New Zealand

From Continental Europe: New Zealand can be reached from most major European cities with one stop in a major Asian city.

Domestic flights. Air New Zealand is the primary domestic carrier, with Quantas and Origin Pacific competing on main trunk routes. Mount Cook Airlines (owned by Air New Zealand) operates mainly from cities to resort areas, and a number of smaller companies serve provincial towns. There are frequent flights from main centers, provincial towns, and resort areas.

Discount Tickets. Before departure, overseas tourists can buy an Air New Zealand air pass, valid for specific periods of travel on domestic airlines. They come to about NZ$150 a flight. Various coach companies offer passes along the routes they operate, either with unlimited stops along a fixed route or a certain number of travel days within a set time-frame. Companies such as Kiwi Experience and Magic Bus offer national coach passes. Members of the Youth Hostel Association are eligible for 15 percent discounts on coaches.

The 'Best of New Zealand' travelpass allows you to explore the country by train, plane, ferry and coach. Using a simple points system called 'Best Points', these travel passes are valid for six months and there is no limit to the number of journeys you can take. It can work out at saving you around 27–31 percent on standard adult fares. For details phone (04) 498-3303 or visit www.bestpass.co.nz

GUIDES and TOURS

A wide choice of escorted package tours is available. These include fly/drive arrangements (with or without accommodation), camper or motor home rentals, fully escorted coach holidays (either North Island, South Island, or both), escorted budget coach holidays, farm holidays, trekking holidays, and ski packages.

"Flightseeing" in light aircraft is one of the pleasures of a New Zealand holiday. It is especially recommended for the outstanding scenic areas of Rotorua, Mt. Cook, the Fox and Franz Josef glaciers, Queenstown, and Milford Sound. Alpine flights use special planes with retractable skis for landing on snow and ice.

H

HEALTH and MEDICAL CARE

Both public and private health services are of a high standard. Hotels and motels usually have a doctor on call, and doctors are listed separately at the front of telephone directories. Medical services are not free, except as a result of an accident, so you should arrange health insurance in advance. New Zealand is without snakes or dangerous wild animals, making it safe for visitors to enjoy outdoor activities. In the case of an accident all visitors are entitled to compensation, which covers reasonable expenses such as doctor's fees and hospitalization. This may severely limit the amount you can recover by legal action against an erring party. And it does not cover illness—insurance is essential. New Zealand has reciprocal health agreements with several countries (including Britain), so check for details before leaving home.

If you've flown a long distance, take it easy for a day or two to get over the jet lag, which is often more pronounced on the second day. Guard against sunburn: Use a sun-screen lotion of at least factor 15 if you're out of doors for any length of time in the summer. Sand flies can be a nuisance, so keep them at bay with insect repellent. The European wasp, with its yellow-and-black striped abdomen, has colonized New Zealand and become a major problem in some bush areas. Trampers should carry anti-histamine medication as a precaution.

Pharmacies (called chemists) are open 9am to 5:30pm Monday to Thursday, until 9pm on Friday, and Saturday morning. The addresses and phone numbers of emergency chemists (for after-hours service) are posted on the doors of all pharmacies.

HITCHHIKING

Inherent risks aside, it's acceptable to hitch a ride. As in most parts of the world, women should not hitchhike alone, nor at night or in isolated places. It's illegal to hitchhike on New Zealand motorways (freeways).

HOLIDAYS

The major public holidays are:

    1 and 2 January   *New Year's*

New Zealand

6 February	*Waitangi Day*
March/April	*Good Friday and Easter Monday*
25 April	*Anzac Day*
June	*Queen's Birthday* (first Monday)
October	*Labour Day* (fourth Monday)
25 and 26 December	*Christmas Day and Boxing Day*

When Christmas, Boxing Day, or New Year's Day falls on a Saturday or Sunday, the public holiday is observed on the following Monday. Also, each province holds a holiday on its own anniversary. These range through the year and can vary, so it's worth checking with an authority such as the New Zealand Tourism Board before you depart.

L

LANGUAGE

Both English and Maori, the language of the indigenous people, are official languages, but English is by far the most commonly spoken. Many place names are in Maori. Pronunciation is not difficult once you master the vowels, which often occur alongside each other but are pronounced separately: *a* as in car; o like "aw" in "paw"; *i* like "ea" in "bean"; *e* as in men; *u* like oo in moon. The only complex sounds are *wh*, pronounced more or less like "f," and *ng*, pronounced like the "ing" in "singing." Syllables are given equal stress.

Here are some of the more common Maori words and phrases you're likely to hear:

ao	cloud	**patu**	club
atua	god	**rangatira**	chief
haere-mai	welcome	**raupo**	bulrush
haere-ra	goodbye	**tangata**	human being
hau	wind	**tangi**	mourning (funeral)
ika	fish	**tapu**	sacred
kai	food	**tohunga**	priest
ka pai	good	**umu**	earth oven
kia ora	good luck	**utu**	satisfaction; revenge
mana	prestige		
maunga	mountain	**wai**	water

moko	tattoo	**waka**	canoe
motu	island	**waiata**	song
pa	fortified village	**whare**	house

If you feel that you've gained a certain proficiency, try one of the longest place-names in the world, attached to a hill in the Hawke's Bay area. In its shortened version it's called *Taumatawhaka-tangihangakoauauota-mateapokaiwhenuakitanatahu*. It means "where Tamatea of the big knees, the man who slid down, climbed, and consumed mountains and is known as the land-eater, played the flute to his beloved."

LAUNDRY and DRY CLEANING

Most motels and some hotels have do-it-yourself laundry facilities. Large hotels provide laundry and dry-cleaning services. At local laundries and dry-cleaners your clothing will usually be returned in 48 hours. You pay a little extra for a same-day or one-hour dry-cleaning rush service.

M

MAPS

Tourist offices and car-rental companies distribute free maps. The New Zealand Automobile Association also produces regional maps and excellent district maps; a nominal sum is charged for North and South Island maps. Wises maps and the Shell road atlas are also well produced and widely available.

MEDIA

New Zealand publishes no daily national newspaper, but main centers have morning dailies. The *New Zealand Herald* (Auckland) and the *Dominion Post* (Wellington) are widely available outside their own areas, as is the *Christchurch Press* on the South Island. Local dailies, usually evening editions, are published in smaller places; they can be bought from news agents, from street-vendors, or from "honesty box" stands, where you drop in the appropriate coins and serve yourself.

The Listener, a weekly newsmagazine, publishes a television and radio guide as well as articles on the arts and social issues. *Metro* and *North and South,* both published in Auckland, provide lively, informative, and topical features. International publications like *Time, Newsweek,* the *Guardian Weekly,* and the *Weekly Telegraph* are widely available.

The better standard hotels may feature CNN on Sky TV; otherwise television consists of four commercial channels, none of which is very exciting. Commercials proliferate, along with many overseas-made repeats and some local content. National Radio (837kHz) is the best radio station for news, current events, and quality programming; numerous other stations cater to all tastes. The BBC World Service is easy to pick up throughout the country, and presents news and current events to a high standard, albeit from a distant part of the planet.

MONEY

Currency. The New Zealand dollar (NZ$) is divided into 100 cents. Notes come in denominations of NZ$5, NZ$10, NZ$20, NZ$50, and NZ$100, and coins in 5c, 10c, 20c, and 50c, and NZ$1 and NZ$2. No restrictions apply to the amount of foreign currency that can be taken in or out of New Zealand.

Banking Hours. 9:30am to 4:30pm Monday to Friday, except public holidays. Some branches are open on Saturday until 12:30pm.

Credit Cards and Traveler's Checks. Internationally recognized credit cards are widely accepted and major currencies such as US dollars, UK pounds, and Australian dollars can be readily changed at banks. Traveler's checks can also be cashed at banks, bigger hotels, and tourist-oriented shops. International credit cards encoded with a PIN number may be used to withdraw cash from automatic teller machines (ATMs), which are widely available in main shopping centers and suburban malls. Check with your bank before departure to ensure this facility is available to you.

O

OPEN HOURS

Decades ago, New Zealand used to close down so utterly on weekends that even trams stopped running, but those days have gone, mercifully. All shops and businesses are open 9am to 5pm Monday to Friday, at least. Most stores are also open on Saturday between 10am and 1pm or later, and many also open on Sunday. In resorts you will find most stores also open in the evenings. Many tourist-oriented stores are open later—until 8pm, for instance—and late-night shopping (until 8pm or 9pm) on Thursday or Friday nights is common. City supermarkets and convenience stores are sometimes open 24 hours. Museums usually open at 9am or 9:30am.

P

POST OFFICES

Main post offices (or post shops, as they are known) offer stationery retailing as well as postal, telegram, and, in many cases, banking services. In rural areas the general store doubles as post office. The hours of operation are 9am to 5pm Monday to Friday and (in large towns and cities only) Saturday 9am to 12:30pm. It costs NZ$1.50 to send postcards or aerograms to anywhere in the world. International airmail envelopes cost NZ$1.50 to Australia and NZ$2.00 to the rest of the world. Domestic mail is divided into first- and second-class levels, as in the UK. The Kiwi version of second-class mail is called Standard; first-class (faster and more expensive) is called FastPost.

PUBLIC TRANSPORTATION

Buses. Local buses run according to a published timetable. Fares are calculated according to the number of "sections" traveled. Some city shuttle buses have "honesty boxes" into which you drop the required amount. (Wellington has electric trains—called "units"—that travel to the northern suburbs.) Coaches provide countryside service. They are not normally air-conditioned, but are heated in winter. Budget-priced backpacker coaches also cover major routes.

Trains. Passenger train services have felt the ax of rationalization in recent years, but four scenic long-distance services remain. Here is a rundown of standard one-way adult fares:

Overlander or **Northerner** (Auckland–Wellington), NZ$145 and NZ$128 respectively.
TranzCoastal (Christchurch–Picton), NZ$81
TranzAlpine (Christchurch–Greymouth), NZ$94 one way or NZ$119 roundtrip.

Inquire about the 'Best of New Zealand 'pass, which can give you travel for up to six months, with unlimited stopovers. The pass entitles holders to travel on the national rail network, as well as on coaches, the Interislander Cook Strait ferries and Air New Zealand (www.bestpass.co.nz).

If you are a member of the Youth Hostels Association (see YOUTH HOSTELS), ask the Association for information about special rail discounts that might be available to you.

Ferries. Interislander car ferries sailing between Wellington and Picton link the North and South islands. The crossing takes three hours; cafeteria and bar facilities are available on board. Express wave-piercing catamaran ferries, taking as little as one hour, operate during the summer—but are canceled if waves get too high. A regular passenger ferry runs from Bluff, the port of Invercargill, to Oban on Stewart Island. Try to book in advance for all ferries, especially during holiday periods. Some sailings are canceled during the low season.

R

RELIGION

New Zealand has no state church, but Christianity is the dominant religion. Protestants outnumber Catholics. The daily papers give details of addresses and times of services. The Yellow Pages of the phone directory in each city list churches and denominations.

T

TELEPHONE

Calls made on private phones are vastly cheaper than those made on public phones. Local calls made from private phones are either free or cost NZ$0.20. Coin-operated phones are rare, although a few remain at airports and rail stations. They accept all coins except 5c pieces. Card-operated public (pay) phones with trunk (toll) and international direct dialing (IDD) are located throughout the country. Cards are readily available in NZ$5, NZ$10, NZ$20, and NZ$50 denominations.

TIME ZONES

New Zealand is 12 hours ahead of Greenwich Mean Time. Clocks advance one hour from the first Sunday in October to the third Sunday in March. The chart below shows the time differences between New Zealand and various cities.

	Los Angeles	New York	London	Sydney	Wellington
Jan	3pm	6pm	11pm	10am	noon
	(Fri)	(Fri)	(Fri)	(Sat)	(Sat)
July	5pm	8pm	1am	10am	noon
	(Fri)	(Fri)	(Sat)	(Sat)	(Sat)

TIPPING

Tipping is a novelty in New Zealand. Tips are given only in appreciation of extra-special service or kindness, at the discretion of visitors. Leaving a few dollars after a meal in a reasonable-quality city restaurant can be appreciated, if the service has been good. Taxi drivers do not expect tips.

Service charges are not added to hotel or restaurant bills—that's the good news. The bad news is that a 12.5 percent Goods and Service Tax (GST) is slapped onto virtually everything. It's usually included in the quoted price—but not always.

TOILETS

Generally labeled "Gentlemen" and "Ladies" or identified by male or female symbols, toilets are found in hotel lobbies, shopping centers, large stores, restaurants, museums, cinemas, and—of course—pubs. Built-up areas have clearly marked public "rest rooms"; they are also located in picnic spots along main roads and at the most frequented beaches.

TOURIST INFORMATION OFFICES

The New Zealand Tourist Board maintains marketing and information offices overseas (the domestic offices do not cater to consumers). There are overseas offices in:

Australia: Level 8, 35 Pitt Street, Sydney, NSW 2000; Tel: (02) 9247-5222.

New Zealand

Hong Kong: 3108 China Merchants Tower, Shun Tak Centre, 168 Connaught Road Central. Tel: (852) 2526-0141.

Japan: World Trade Center Building 12F, 2-4-1, Hamamatsu -cho, Minato-ku, Tokyo 105-6112; Tel: (03) 5400-1311.

Singapore: 391 Orchard Road, #15-01 Ngee Ann City, 15th floor, Tower A, 0923; Tel: 738-5844.

UK: New Zealand House, Haymarket, London SW1Y 4TQ; Tel: (020) 7930-1662.

US: Suite 300, 501 Santa Monica Blvd., Santa Monica, CA 90401; Tel: (310) 395-7480.

New Zealand embassies abroad can sometimes supply travel information, although this service may be limited.

Visitor Information Centers dispense tourist information in most towns throughout New Zealand.

W

WEIGHTS and MEASURES

The Metric System is used throughout New Zealand.

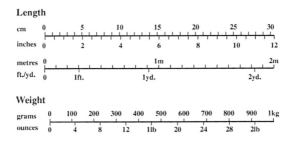

Temperature

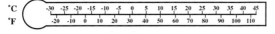

Y

YOUTH HOSTELS

Accommodation at backpacker hostels starts from about NZ$15 a night for a shared room in an establishment with laundry facilities. Backpacker hostels, which exist in most cities and tourist-region towns, provide clean, tidy lodgings, ranging from four-bed cabins and small hotels to bunk rooms and 300-bed accommodation centers. Common living rooms add a friendly touch. Free guides are available at information centers. Booking ahead is essential in December and January and advisable during the rest of summer.

YHA New Zealand is part of the worldwide YHA hosteling group. It runs 64 hostels throughout New Zealand, including properties near National Parks, ski fields, and popular walking tracks. In the cities, YHA hostels are modern and centrally located.

There is no age limit and there are no curfews. Properties usually offer separate sleeping and bathroom facilities for males and females, although some feature single and family accommodation. Reduced rates apply for guests aged under 18. Non-members may stay at manager's discretion and are charged more than members. The YHA is well worth joining, as it gives a huge range of travel discounts, including 15 percent discount on coach fares. YHA New Zealand can issue overseas visitors who are not current members with a Hostelling International Card, valid for 12 months throughout the world. It costs NZ$30 for the whole card or can be bought in installments of NZ$3 per night.

For details, write to Freepost YHA Membership Administration, YHA New Zealand National Office, PO Box 436, Christchurch, New Zealand; Tel: (03) 3799970; fax: (03) 365-4476; e-mail info@yha.org.nz; www.stayyha.com.

Recommended Hotels

Accommodation in New Zealand range from five-star city hotels and luxury country lodges to low-cost backpacker hostels. The country's top hotels—all the well-known chains are represented—are comparable to those anywhere in the world. Serviced apartments and all-suite hotels start from about NZ$700 a week. Luxury lodges, usually compact and distinctive mansions or custom-designed villas of exceptional quality, offer world-class service and sublime surroundings at between NZ$175 and NZ$700 a night. Backpackers are served by more than 250 hostels, some in settings that are just as splendid as those enjoyed by more expensive establishments; rates start at NZ$10 per person for a shared room (see Youth Hostels on page 129).

The big accommodation story in recent years has been the proliferation of bed-and-breakfast properties and boutique hotels. These range from grand, historic houses to suburban family homes.

The following price guidelines—for a double room with bath—are approximate only, as many hotels offer specials and rates fluctuate.

$$$$$	above NZ$240
$$$$	NZ$180–NZ$240
$$$	NZ$100–NZ$180
$$	NZ$60–NZ$100
$	below NZ$60

THE NORTH ISLAND

Auckland

Auckland International YHA Hostel $ *1-35 Turner St.; Tel: (09) 302-8200; fax: (09) 302-8205.* One of Auckland's largest youth hostels offers state-of-the-art, eco-friendly accommodation. No duties. Rooms with bath. Open 24 hours. Wheelchair access. 174 beds.

Devonport Villa Inn $$$–$$$$ *46 Tainui Rd., Devonport; Tel: (09) 445-8397; fax: (09) 445-9766; www.devonport villa.inn.co.nz.* Full of Edwardian charm, this award-winning B&B in an historic timber home is just a 15-minute stroll from Devonport village and an 8-minute ferry ride (across the harbor) from downtown Auckland. 7 rooms all with en-suites.

Gulf Harbour Lodge $$$$$ *Harbour Village Dr., Whangaparaoa Peninsula; Tel: (09) 428-1118; fax: (09) 428-1119.* On Hauraki Gulf 45 minutes north of the city, this canal-side lodge has a distinctly Mediterranean feel. Country Club facilities, include golf course, tennis and squash courts, heated pool, and gymnasium. Wheelchair access. 35 rooms.

Ascot Metropolis $$$$ *1 Carthouse Lane, Tel: (09) 300-8800;* In the heart of Auckland, the Ascott Metropolis combines the influences of cosmopolitan Manhatten and Chicago. Elegant one and two bedroom suites offer unashamed luxury with separate living and dining areas, designer kitchen and breathtaking harbour views.

Sheraton Auckland Hotel and Towers $$$$$ *83 Symonds St; Tel: (09) 379-5132; fax: (09) 377-9367; www.sheraton.com \auckland.* A luxurious 5-star experience. Wheelchair access. 410 rooms.

Sky City $$$$ *Victoria and Federal streets; Tel: (09) 912-6000; fax: (09) 363-6388; www.skycity.co.nz.* International-style hotel with modern rooms, many of which overlook the harbor. Part of the casino complex. Wheelchair access. 344 rooms.

Waitakere Park Lodge $$$ *573 Scenic Drive; Tel: (09) 814-9622; www.waitakereparklodge.co.nz.* A private paradise surrounded by rainforest perched 244 km (800 feet) above sea level. Within easy reach of the city center, 17 suites with modern facilites, a library and Kauri lounge.

Bay of Islands
Aloha Seaview Resort $$$ *32-36 Seaview Rd., Paihia; Tel:*

(09) 402-7540; fax: (09) 402-7820. Self-contained one- and two-bedroom apartments in two hectares of native bush and sub-tropical garden. Peaceful atmosphere with breathtaking sea views, but only a short walk to the shops and waterfront of Paihia. Wheelchair access. 20 rooms.

Kingfish Lodge Resort \$\$\$\$\$ *Whangaroa Harbour, Northland; Tel: (09) 405-0164; fax: (09) 405-0163; www.kingfishlodge.co.nz.* 30 minutes from Kerikeri, this secluded lodge is accessible only by sea or air. All rooms are near the water's edge and spectacular views of fjord-like scenery (from private balconies). Diving and canoeing, year-round sport fishing, and sightseeing and winery cruises. Kingfish Bar; plenty of fresh local seafood in the restaurant. 12 rooms.

Orongo Bay Homestead \$\$\$–\$\$\$\$ *Aucks Rd., RD 1, Russell; Tel: (09) 403-7527; fax: (09) 403-7675; www.thehomestead.co.nz.* Built around 1860, this was New Zealand's first American Consulate. Seventeen acres of lawns and native bush with views to the Bay of Islands, organic cuisine and a chef who has twice won the NZ Food and Travel Award. Wheelchair access. 4 rooms.

Peppertree Lodge \$ *15 Kings Rd., Paihia; Tel: and fax: (09) 402-6122.* Clean, well-equipped hostel with great communal areas. Dorm or double rooms. Wheelchair access. 64 beds.

Rotorua

Hot Rock Backpackers \$ *1286 Arawa St.; Tel: (07) 347-9469; fax: (07) 348-8616.* A highly-rated backpacker lodge with spacious thermally-heated rooms, friendly helpful staff, and three pools. Wheelchair access. 150 beds.

Huka Lodge \$\$\$\$\$ *Huka Falls Road, Taupo; Tel: (07) 378-5791; fax: (07) 378-0427; www.hukalodge.co.nz.* The very height of understated luxury (Queen Elizabeth has stayed here), this 1920s lodge is on park-like grounds just above the Huka Falls, an hour from Rotorua. Individual suites among trees bordering the Waikato River. Regularly rated as one of the best hotels in the world. Fine restaurant. Wheelchair access. 20 suites.

Royal Lakeside Novotel $$$$ *Lake End, Tutanekai St.; Tel: (07) 346-3888; fax: (07) 347-1888.* This hotel promises commanding views and regal treatment. Facilities include a spa and fitness center with geothermal pools. Wheelchair access. 199 rooms.

Solitaire Lodge $$$$$ *Lake Tarawera; Tel: (07) 362-8208; fax: (07) 362-8448.* Nestled in bushland on a private peninsula 25 minutes from Rotorua, this luxurious lodge has panoramic views over the lake and beyond to Mount Tarawera. 10 suites.

Wylie Court Motor Lodge $$$ *345 Fenton St.; Tel: (07) 347-7879; fax: (07) 346-1494.* Standard and executive suites, outdoor heated swimming pool set in two acres of gardens, and a restaurant open 7 days. Wheelchair access. 36 units.

Wellington

Hotel Rafaele $$$ *360 Oriental Bay; Tel: (04) 384-3450; fax: (04) 384-3652.* Situated on the popular waterfront promenade, every room in this hotel has a private balcony with a spectacular harbor view. Wheelchair access. 63 rooms.

James Cook Hotel Grand Chancellor $$$$ *147 The Terrace; Tel: (04) 499-9500; fax: (04) 499-9800;* www.grandchancellor.co.nz. With entrances on both the Terrace and Lambton Quay, this luxurious hotel straddles the premier shopping precinct and the principal commercial districts. Wheelchair access. 260 rooms.

Hotel Intercontinental $$$$$ *Grey and Featherston streets; Tel: (04) 472-2722; fax: (04) 472-4724;* www.interconti.com. Wellington's leading international hotel, in the heart of the Central Business District. Dining options to suit all tastes, from Tex-Mex to haute cuisine. Wheelchair access. 233 rooms and a fitness center with a heated pool.

Wharekauhau Country Estate $$$$$ *Western Lake Rd., RD 3, Featherston, Pirinoa; Tel: (06) 307-7581; fax: (06) 307-7799; www.wharekauhau.co.nz.* Pronounced "Forry-*ko*-ho," this premier lodge sits on a sweeping expanse of ruggedly beautiful land along Palliser Bay, a 90-minute drive east of Wellington. Three-time winner of the prestigious Andrew Harper Hideaway Award for Country House Hotel of the Year. Modeled on an Edwardian country mansion, the main house boasts a Grand Hall, massive fireplaces, and sumptuous furnishings. Elegant cottage suites have fireplaces and spectacular views of the ocean. Both classic French cuisine and simple country fare. Wheelchair access. 12 double suites; 1 single.

THE SOUTH ISLAND

Christchurch

Crowne Plaza Christchurch $$$$$ *Kilmore and Durham streets; Tel: (03) 365-7799; fax: (03) 365-0082; www.christchurch.crowneplaza.com.* This premier hotel is also one of the city's most striking modern buildings. Offers all the luxuries and great views over "the garden city." Wheelchair access. 298 rooms.

The George $$$$$ *50 Park Terrace; Tel: (03) 379-4560; fax: (03) 366-6747; www.thegeorge.com.* This luxurious boutique hotel, minutes from the center of the city, has park and river views. Situated in the heart of the "culture zone," with the historic arts center, museum, casino, and theaters within walking distance. Wheelchair access. 57 rooms.

Heritage Christchurch $$$ *24-28 Cathedral Square; Tel: (03) 377-9722; fax: (03) 377-9881; www.heritagehotels.co.nz.* Guests can choose to stay in the modern Heritage Tower, or in a turn-of-the-century building that has retained its historic charm. Wheelchair access. 176 rooms.

Rolleston House YHA Hostel $ *5 Worcester Blvd.; Tel: (03) 366-6564; fax: (03) 365-5589.* Turn-of-the-century home converted into backpacker lodging. Across from the lovely historic Arts Centre with its weekend craft markets. 52 beds.

Dunedin

Motel Moray Place **$$** *97 Moray Pl.; Tel: (03) 477-2050; fax: (03) 477-1991.* The most centrally located motel in Dunedin, built in 1996. Friendly hosts and spacious well-equipped units. Wheelchair access. 40 units.

Quality Hotel Dunedin **$$$** *Upper Moray Pl.; Tel: (03) 477-6784; fax: (03) 474-0115.* Centrally located on the edge of the Octagon. All rooms have balconies with views of the city. Wheelchair access. 55 rooms.

Southern Cross Hotel **$$$$** *Princes and High streets; Tel: (03) 477-0752; fax: (03) 477-5776.* Dunedin's largest hotel, in the heart of the business district. Two licensed restaurants, a deli, two bars, a fitness center and a casino. Wheelchair access. 178 rooms.

Stafford Gables YHA Hostel **$** *71 Stafford St.; Tel: and fax: (03) 474-1919.* A turn-of-the-century former hospital, just a 10-minute walk from the Octagon. Large rooms, including some family rooms, and balconies. 64 beds.

Nelson

Cathedral Inn **$$$** *369 Trafalgar St. S.; Tel: (03) 548-7369; fax: (03) 548-0369.* Just behind the cathedral in the heart of the city, this 120-year-old manor surrounded by trees has been renovated to retain its charm but provide every modern comfort. Hearty breakfasts. 7 rooms.

Rutherford Hotel **$$$** *Nile St. W.; Tel: (03) 548-2299; fax: (03) 546-3003.* Top-of-the-range accommodation in a hotel equipped with swimming pool, spa, and gym. Wheelchair access. 114 rooms.

Kimi Ora Spa Resort **$$–$$$$** *Kaiteriteri, Tel: 0508-546-4672; www.kimiora.co.nz.* Twenty Swiss-style chalet apartments with seaviews. Features a health centre with pool, sauna, spa, steam room, tennis courts and an extensive range of spa treatments. Fully licensed wholefood restaurant.

Hotel d'Urville $$$$$ *52 Queen St., Blenheim; Tel: (03) 577-9945; fax: (03) 577-9946; www.durville.com.* Situated within an historic building in the town center, this boutique hotel has a reputation for unstuffy elegance. Luxurious, individually themed rooms. The d'Urville Wine Bar and Brasserie is open for breakfast, lunch, and dinner. Wheelchair access. 11 rooms.

Nelson Central YHA $ *59 Rutherford St.; Tel: (03) 545-9988; fax: (03) 545-9989.* This custom-built hostel is widely acknowledged to be the best in town. Excellent facilities and friendly, helpful staff. Wheelchair access. 30 rooms.

Queenstown

Millbrook Resort $$$$$ *Malaghans Rd.; Tel: (03) 441-7000; fax: (03) 441-7007; www.millbrook.co.nz.* Situated between Queenstown and Arrowtown, this multi-award-winning resort provides luxurious modern accommodation in restored historic buildings. Among many attractions are an 18-hole golf course designed by Bob Charles and spectacular alpine views.

The Millennium $$$$$ *Frankton Rd. and Stanley St.; Tel: (03) 441-8888; fax: (03) 441-8889;* www.mcqhotels.co.nz. Built in 1995, this centrally located luxury hotel lacks lake views but has excellent facilities. In summer it offers Queenstown's only air-conditioned rooms. Wheelchair access. 220 rooms.

Queenstown House $$$ *69 Hallenstein St.; Tel: (03) 442-9043; fax: (03) 442-8744.* A unique small hotel with magnificent lake and mountain views from every room, and a hostess who is a local personality. Complimentary New Zealand wines and cheese each evening before dinner. 14 rooms.

Queenstown YHA Hostel $ *88/90 Lake Esplanade; Tel: (03) 442-8413; fax: (03) 442-6561.* Large and bustling hostel on the lakefront, a 10-minute walk from the town center. Offers fabulous views at a budget price. Facilities for drying and storing skis and snow-boards. Wheelchair access. 150 beds.

Recommended Restaurants

New Zealand is singularly blessed when it comes to food: It possesses high-quality natural ingredients (the foundation of fine dining everywhere) in great abundance—fresh fruits and vegetables, an enviable range of freshwater and saltwater fish, game, and farmed meat of all types.

Subtle and distinctive tastes are evolving into a recognizable national style that incorporates influences from California and Asia as well as hints of French nouvelle cuisine. The new buzz is "Pacific Rim" cooking, which combines such staples as steak, salmon, and shellfish with accompaniments like sun dried tomatoes, lemongrass, coconut, basil, ginger, and exotic fruits. On the fruit front, you may encounter the tamarillo (which used to be called a tree tomato) and the kiwifruit (once known as a Chinese gooseberry). Lime-juice and banana join forces with vegetables like kumara (native sweet potato) and pumpkin. Farmed venison (marketed as cervena) makes regular appearances.

While few restaurants serve a three-course meal for under NZ$35, there are plenty of less expensive options. (Servings are often hearty, and in many places a main course is often enough.) Sandwich cafés are widespread, serving healthy and tasty open sandwiches for between NZ$5 and NZ$10 (they often use New Zealand's Vogel bread, to which many visitors quickly become addicted). Chain hamburger bars abound, with burgers generally costing between NZ$3.50 and NZ$5. (See also Eating Out on page 100)

The price guidelines below are based on an average three-course meal for one person without drinks.

$$$$	above NZ$40
$$$	NZ$30–NZ$40
$$	NZ$20–NZ$30
$	below NZ$20

THE NORTH ISLAND

Auckland

Andiamo $$–$$$ *194 Jervois Road, Jervois Bay.* Popular eatery, generous portions, modern cuisine and good hearty breakfasts. Indoor and outdoor dining available.

Antoine's Restaurant $$$$ *333 Parnell Rd., Parnell; Tel: (09) 379-8756.* One of Auckland's most prestigious restaurants, serving fine French cuisine in the up-market village of Parnell. Open for lunch Mon–Fri, dinner Mon–Sat. Reservations essential.

Harbourside Seafood Bar and Grill $$$$ *1st floor, Ferry Building, Quay St.; Tel: (09) 307-0556.* Up-market dining on the waterfront. Deliciously prepared, super-fresh seafood. Try the Trio—hapuka, kingfish, and salmon in one succulent dish. Great views of the harbour.

Orbit Sky Tower $$$ *Victoria and Federal streets, Tel: (09) 912-6000.* A unique dining experience. This fine restaurant, serving á-la-carte brasserie-style New Zealand cuisine, stands 190 m (623 ft) above the ground atop the tallest structure in the city and revolves very slowly, affording ever-changing views.

Porterhouse Blue $$ *58 Calliope Rd., Devonport; Tel: (09) 445-0309.* This celebrated restaurant in the village of Devonport is an eight-minute ferry ride across the water from Auckland; a courtesy bus transfers guests from the wharf.

Rice $-$$ *10-12 Federal Street, CBD; Tel: (09) 359-9113; www.rice.co.nz.* International cuisine. Mouth-watering recipes derived from 20 types or derivates of rice. Modern and chic, with a stylish bar attached. Try the entrée platter, especially the BBQ pork and crispy vermicelli witlof bites.

SPQR $$$ *150 Ponsonby Rd., Ponsonby; Tel: (09) 360-1170.* One of Auckland's most famous and loved restaurants. Great cuisine, especially the linguine and clams dish. Popular at night.

Bay of Islands

Bistro 40/Only Seafood $$$ *40 Marsden Rd., Paihia; Tel: (09) 402-7444.* One restaurant sits above the other in this superb water-front location. The bistro specializes in fine NZ cuisine, with an accent on meat and game; Only Seafood is true to its name. Good selection of quality New Zealand wines. Open daily for dinner.

Café Over The Bay $–$$ *Upstairs at The Mall, Marsden Rd., Paihia; Tel: (09) 402-8147.* Enjoy an early morning breakfast on a balcony overlooking the glorious Bay of Islands. A healthy menu, with plenty of vegetarian options, and muffins and cakes fresh-baked on the premises daily. Open 8am; dinner Oct–April.

Gannets Restaurant $$$$ *Town Sq., Russell; Tel: (09) 403-7990.* Recommended by locals, Gannets offers a varied menu with plenty of seafood. Everything is homemade, including the ice cream. Open for dinner every day except Monday.

Twin Pines Restaurant and Bar $$ *Tel: (09) 402-7195.* Adjacent to Haruru Falls, the historic Twin Pines focuses strongly on local products. Features an extensive wine cellar.

The Duke of Marlborough $$$$ *The Strand, Russell; Tel: (09) 403-7829; www.theduke.co.nz.* The menu in this boutique hotel has French foundations, but the New Zealand influences are strong. Local oysters and mussels are brought straight from the sea to the table. The Northland beef is commendable.

York Street Café $–$$ *1 York St., Russell; Tel: (09) 403-7360.* Fresh local food at reasonable prices. The chowder is widely praised. Several vegetarian options as well. Open daily 10am–10pm.

Rotorua
The Landing Cafe $$ *Lake Tarawera, Tel: (07) 362-8595.*

New Zealand

Nestled on the shores of Lake Tarawera, this world-famous cafe is heavily themed on local attractions. Mouth-watering fare and open fires in the winter.

Poppy's Villa $$$$ *4 Marguerita St.; Tel: (07) 347-1700.* A very popular restaurant with a menu dominated by award-winning beef and lamb dishes. Housed in an Edwardian villa a few minutes drive from the city center. Open seven nights for dinner. Reservations recommended.

Rendezvous Restaurant $$$ *1282 Hinemoa St.; Tel: (07) 348-9273.* A comprehensive á la carte menu. The signature dish involves a lightly smoked rack of lamb coated with herb butter and sesame seeds. Open for dinner Tue–Sat. Reservations advised.

Sirocco $$ *1280 Eruera Street; Tel: (07) 347 3388.* Mainly Mediterranean, with a reputation for formal Italian cuisine. Located opposite Rotorua's cinema complex, this café-style restaurant is recommended for either meals or light snacks.

Wellington

The Boulcott Street Bistro $$$$ *99 Boulcott St.; Tel: (04) 499-4199.* A pretty cottage just off Willis Street houses this fine restaurant, which has an air of relaxed formality. New Zealand's finest game and seafood imaginatively prepared and served with grace and style. Open for lunch Mon–Fri, dinner Mon–Sat.

Brava $$ *2 Courtenay Place, Tel: (04) 384-1159.* A popular restaurant with an excellent breakfast menu and inspiring cuisine. Politicians, actors and film stars have been spotted in this restaurant which is located beneath Downstage Theatre.

The Lido $–$$ *Wakefield and Victoria streets; Tel: (04) 499-6666.* A Wellington institution, this centrally located café with sidewalk tables and a "fishbowl" character is a great spot for watching the world walk by. Delicious snacks and meals in generous portions.

The Martinborough Bistro $$$–$$$$ *Kitchener St. and Memorial Sq., Martinborough; Tel: (06) 306-9350.* A magnificently restored small country hotel houses this upscale restaurant with a reputation for excellently prepared and presented cuisine. The menu is influenced by French/Mediterranean traditions. Wellingtonians come to stay for the weekend and tour the wineries encircling the town of Martinborough. Reservations advised.

Logan Brown Restaurant $–$$ *192 Cuba Street; tel: (04) 801-5114.* Book in advance to secure a table at arguably the city's hottest restaurant.

Parade Café $–$$ *148 Oriental Parade; Tel: (04) 385-3931.* Busy, popular café and restaurant ideally situated to top off a promenade around the seafront. An open fire in winter, and a sunny courtyard in summer. Great food, reasonable prices, eclectic ambiance.

Shed 5 $$$–$$$$ *Queens Wharf; Tel: (04) 499-9069.* Smart seafood by the water in a well-renovated 1880s wool shed, which is café, bar, and restaurant in one with room to spare. The menu includes meats as well. Popular for relaxed, extended corporate lunches.

THE SOUTH ISLAND

Christchurch

Dux de Lux $–$$ *Arts Centre, Hereford and Montreal streets; Tel: (03) 366-6919.* A popular restaurant and bar, with a huge open courtyard, award-winning beer, and live music. Tuesday nights is jazz night. A big, eclectic menu with lots of fresh local seafood.

Il Felice $–$$ *56 Lichfield Street; Tel: (03) 366-7535.* A very popular Italian BYO restaurant. The owners pride themselves in recreating the full Italian experience from fresh pasta to passionate ambience.

Saggio di'Vino $$$ *Victoria St. and Bealey Ave.; Tel: (03) 379-4006.* A full-fledged "vinotheque"—where the food is designed to complement the 80-some wines that are offered by the glass. Open daily for dinner.

Sign of the Takahe $$$$ *Dyers Pass and Hackthorne Rd., Cashmere Hills; Tel: (03) 332-4052.* Silver service and fine dining in a baronial hilltop castle. This unique restaurant offers modern and traditional New Zealand cuisine. Reserve well in advance.

Retour $$$$ *Cambridge Terrace and Manchester St.; Tel: (03) 365-2888.* Formerly a band rotunda, now a glass-sided restaurant in an excellent position overlooking the Avon River. Perfect for a romantic lunch or dinner, it specializes in premium New Zealand cuisine. Open daily for dinner except Monday between April–Sept.

Dunedin

Bell Pepper Blues $$$$ *474 Princes St.; Tel: (03) 474-0973.* Widely rated one of Dunedin's best restaurants, delivering state-of-the-art Pacific rim dishes based on the finest New Zealand fish and game. Open Mon–Sat for dinner. Wed–Fri for lunch.

A Cow Called Bertha $$$ *199 Upper Stuart St.; Tel: (03) 477-2993.* Swiss-style country cuisine. A variety of meat dishes with the emphasis on big flavors and sauces. Open Mon–Sat for dinner.

Etrusco at the Savoy $$ *Savoy Building, 8a Moray Pl.; Tel: (03) 477-3737.* Casual and friendly Italian restaurant, where the low prices belie the quality of the food. Set in a beautifully restored, high-ceiling building just off the Octagon. Open daily for dinner.

The Palms Restaurant $$$ *18 Queens Gardens; Tel: (03) 477-6534.* Popular with the locals, this elegant, relaxed restaurant serves up generous portions from a varied menu. Enjoy lovely views over the Queens Gardens (on summer evenings) from the huge windows of this spacious turn-of-the-century building. Open daily for dinner.

Ombrellos $$ *10 Clarendon Street; Tel: (03) 477-8773.* Highly imaginative cuisine in an attractive, wood-panelled interior. Excellent wine list.

Nelson

The Boatshed $$$ *350 Wakefield Quay; Tel: (03) 546-9783.* This enormously popular restaurant sits out over the water on stilts and offers glorious sunset views over Tasman Bay. The seafood is superb and the prices are very reasonable.

Broccoli Row $–$$ *5 Buxton Square; Tel: (03) 548-9621.* A popular and highly recommended vegetarian restaurant. Generous portions, daily specials, and courtyard dining. Open Aug–June for lunch and dinner. Reservations essential for dinner.

Chez Eelco $ *296 Trafalgar St.; Tel: (03) 548-7595.* At the foot of the cathedral steps, this café has been a Nelson institution for several decades. Try the excellent mussel chowder. Open daily 6am–9pm.

Ciao $$$ *94 Collingwood St.; Tel: (03) 548-9874.* A comprehensive menu of "international fusion" dishes using excellent local products. Only organic ingredients are used where possible. Highly recommended by the locals. Open Mon–Sat for dinner.

Suter Art Gallery Restaurant $$–$$$$ *208 Bridge St.; Tel: (03) 548-4040.* This café and restaurant, which offers views of the Botanical Gardens from large windows, serves "New English" cuisine — New Zealand food with European roots. Open daily year-round for lunch; dinner Sept–Mar Thur–Mon.

Twelve Trees $$ *Allan Scott Wines and Estate, Jacksons Rd., Blenheim; Tel: (03) 572-7123.* A winery restaurant with a menu to perfectly accent Allan Scott's full-bodied wines. Gorgeous indoor/outdoor setting seven minutes out of town toward the airport. Open daily year-round for lunch, dinner Dec–April.

Queenstown

The Bunker $$ *Cow Lane; Tel: (03) 441-8030.* Small, stylish restaurant serving simple, fresh, modern cuisine. Reservations advised. Open daily for dinner.

Lone Star $$ *14 Brecon Street; Tel: (03) 442-9995.* As the name implies, a Western-style restaurant. Good food and huge portions.

Minami Jujisei *45 Beach Street; Tel: (03) 442-9854.* Award-winning Japanese cuisine; particularly good for those who have never tried Japanese food before. Traditional cuisine mixed with modern influences.

Roaring Megs Restaurant $$$ *57 Shotover St.; Tel: (03) 442-9676.* A renovated gold-miner's cottage turned fine restaurant. The house specialty is an award-winning rack of lamb. Open daily for dinner.

Winnie Bagoes $–$$ *7-9 The Mall; Tel: (03) 442-8635.* Lively bar and restaurant with a reputation for delicious gourmet pizza and pasta. Predictably popular with backpackers. Happy hours, pool tables, occasional live music.

Bell Pepper Blues $$ *474 Princes Street; Tel: (03) 474-0973.* Pleasant, high-quality restaurant with fireside atmosphere and outstanding food. Always very full.

INDEX